Walking The Red Road: Empowering Practices for Your Spiritual Journey

Larry Running Turtle Salazar and Pamela Two Spirits Reader

Published by 2 Spirits Press, 2024.

WALKING THE RED ROAD: EMPOWERING PRACTICES FOR YOUR SPIRITUAL JOURNEY

First edition. April 22, 2024.

Copyright © 2024 Larry Running Turtle Salazar and Pamela Two Spirits Reader.

ISBN: 979-8990266414

Written by Larry Running Turtle Salazar and Pamela Two Spirits Reader.

Table of Contents

This book is dedicated to our spouses. Patsy Salazar and David Reader who tirelessly support all our endeavors. We love you to the moon and back.

ACKNOWLEDGMENTS

To Patsy, without whose tireless dedication and support in life, this book would not have been possible. And to my family who continue to support my endeavors: my daughters, Yvette Darlene Yellow Bear and Yvonne Starlene Rising Star; my brothers, Ernest and Jesse; and my sisters Judy, Brenda, Tammy, Rosemary, Joanne, Cat, Connie, and my granddaughter MadalynMargot Salazar-Gomez Butterfly Woman. And last but not least, a special thank you to my co author and sister Pamela Two Spirits Reader and her hardworking editor and loving husband David "Spock" Reader.

— Larry Running Turtle Salazar

In Love

The sun penetrates my body, and I feel warm inside.
The wind pulsates through me, and I feel my breath quicken.
The water caresses me into a hypnotic state,
and I am one no more.
I am webbed with my relations as the ancestors whisper in the wind.
Thank you Mother Earth, Father Sky, and Grandmother Water
for every molecule you embrace with me.
— Pamela Two Spirits Reader

FORWARD

I admired Larry Running Turtle Salazar from the first time we met almost 20 years ago. Larry Running Turtle's unwavering faith illuminates his path, casting a radiant light on his journey towards fulfillment and purpose. With each step, he courageously moves forward, guided by the wisdom of his ancestors and the teachings of the Good Red Road. With a passion for sharing knowledge and teachings, Larry gives himself freely to all people. His achievements are widely recognized and extensively documented. Many of his empowering stories and journeys will be revealed in this book.

My healing journey is based on a powerful dream by my spirit guide "Clap Dance" who led me to my profession as a hospice nurse. The transformative ceremonies of Clap Dance have been instrumental in shaping my healing journey, propelling me towards new realms of self-discovery and leading me to pursue a path as a counselor, hypnotherapist and Reiki practitioner. In my dreams, I consistently experience a profound sense of interconnectedness, recognizing the divine unity that binds us all together in a sacred web of existence.

We wrote our first book, *The Pipe and the Pen* in 4 months as a fundraiser supporting a native monument and ceremonial space called the Ishka Sacred Site in Corpus Christi, Texas. The Ishka Site is the inspiration of Larry Running Turtle, who is not only the primary motivator behind the project, but has tirelessly dedicated his life's work to the project. This includes a march that he has led every year since 1997 (except the pandemic year) to bring awareness to this cause. There's more detail below in the story of Larry Running Turtle. To view the entire proposal of the ISHKA project, including pictures and how to donate, please refer to the endnotes of this book.

We were ecstatic when Larry sold all 1,500 copies of our first book at the store where he works in Corpus Christi, Texas. Unfortunately, the publishing company went out of business and he could not obtain any more books. We are beyond grateful to all of you and your persistence for wanting a second book! Our new book, *Walking the Red Road*, includes more detailed lessons of the original book and additional chapters. We explain how to gather your spiritual medicines and end the book with teachings on how to remove blockages in order to manifest your soul's purpose. And, as always, we want you to know how loved and awesome you are in so many ways!

Walking the Red Road blends heartfelt teachings of a Native American brother and a white adopted sister. It entails original instructions and spiritual medicines from Native American, Buddhist, and Christian philosophies as well as other spiritual teachings. We mirror those teachings with personal examples to help you realize you are not alone on this journey. Our wish is that you will awaken to the sacredness in everything around you, and to take responsibility for honoring yourself as sacred as well. This book emphasizes loving each other as brothers and sisters, honoring Mother Earth, opening your heart to Creator, and understanding the connectedness of all things.

In this book, we refer to the concept of God as the Christ Consciousness, Collective Consciousness, Creator, the Buddha Mind, Yahweh, Wakan Tanka, The Great Mystery, the Great Spirit, or the spirit that lives in all. There are many more concepts for God and we honor them all, and are not making any judgement. We include all faiths, including agnostic, in our circle of friends, and we do not intend to isolate or favor anyone. Rooted in Native American concepts and beliefs, this book often refers to God as the Creator and the Great Spirit present in ALL things.

Both authors have blended their teachings in this book, acknowledging that they wrote most of it with one voice. *Walking The Red Road* is just the tip of the iceberg among many teachings and books that are out there, and we encourage you to pick up one that resonates with you. Our belief is that we are part of Creator, the Collective and Christ Consciousness, Mother Earth and her children; the stars, the trees, and the land. See the light of God within you and embrace the simple teachings in this book to further encourage and inspire you to connect to infinite love.

Ishka (until we meet again)

Pamela Two Spirits Reader, Florida

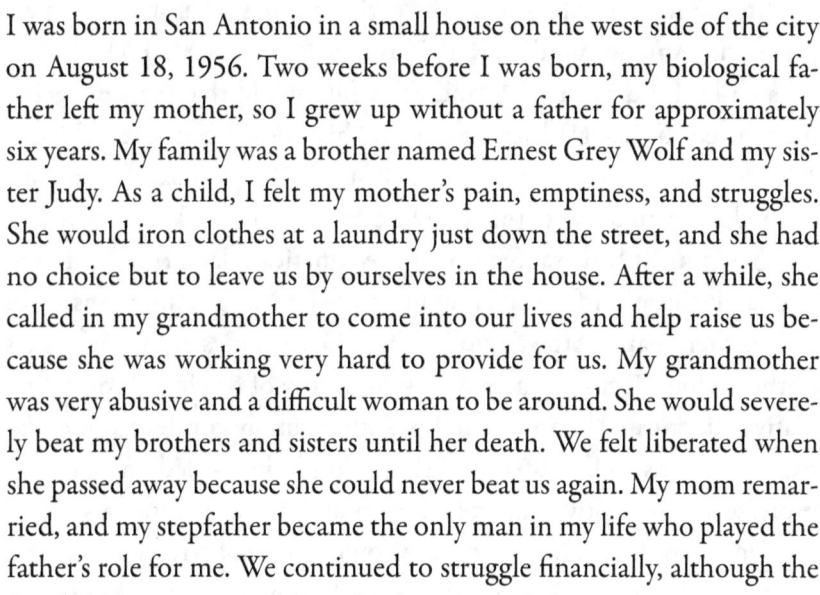

OUR STORIES

The Journey of Larry Running Turtle Salazar

I was born in San Antonio in a small house on the west side of the city on August 18, 1956. Two weeks before I was born, my biological father left my mother, so I grew up without a father for approximately six years. My family was a brother named Ernest Grey Wolf and my sister Judy. As a child, I felt my mother's pain, emptiness, and struggles. She would iron clothes at a laundry just down the street, and she had no choice but to leave us by ourselves in the house. After a while, she called in my grandmother to come into our lives and help raise us because she was working very hard to provide for us. My grandmother was very abusive and a difficult woman to be around. She would severely beat my brothers and sisters until her death. We felt liberated when she passed away because she could never beat us again. My mom remarried, and my stepfather became the only man in my life who played the father's role for me. We continued to struggle financially, although the family became more stable with a loving stepfather.

When I was about six years old, there was a martial arts school across from where we lived. I used to hang around out front, but the instructor would not let me come in. He felt I needed to have my parents with me at the school, but my parents were working and didn't have the time. So I would cross the street and hang around by the door or window and watch him train his students. In those days, martial arts training was secretive and not the popular stuff you see on movies and TV

7

shows. I was fascinated, and I knew I wanted to engage in martial arts training. When I turned seven, the instructor finally let me come inside and study. Soon after I started training, my family moved to Corpus Christi, but my parents sent me to stay with our relatives in San Antonio every summer so I could study. During my summer training, I was to do things that were secretive and difficult, and I learned special skills and a spiritual perspective that has helped me throughout my life.

Growing up in Corpus Christi was very difficult for a young Native American. We did not even have the inherent right, unlike other American citizens, to religious freedom. Some of our ceremonies were not legal to perform until I was in my early twenties when the Congress passed the American Indian Religious Freedom Act (AIRFA) in 1978. As a child, I did not understand the white world that we were being introduced to. Later, I learned that the historical treatment of Native Americans in Texas differs from most states. When Texas became independent from Mexico, the Republic of Texas realized that the Mexican government had granted no Native Americans land titles and used that as justification for expelling most of the Native Americans from the northern parts of the republic. The primary duties in the early years of the famous Texas Rangers consisted mostly of driving off or killing Native Americans. In Southern Texas, they simply considered the Native Americans to be Mexicans. They deported or killed anyone who professed to be Native American. Even after Texas became a state in the Union, the federal government could not make treaties with the remaining Native Americans. The state of Texas adamantly refused to contribute public land for reservations. After I enrolled in first grade in Corpus Christi, they immediately took me to the school office. They sat me down, and the principal came out with a pair of clippers and completely shaved my head. That haircut was the start of my identity crisis of living in two different worlds. During the day, I would come to school and play the part of a Hispanic boy even though I didn't even speak Spanish. Our family had taken Hispanic surnames as "survival" names and outwardly blended into the TexMex culture.

Over the intervening years, this Mexican/Catholic cultural lens has filtered our Native stories and traditions. Our people had assumed the identity to keep from being expelled from our land, or killed. We could not speak Apache in school, only English. When I came home from school, my mom would teach us our Native culture. She showed us how to raise animals and dress a hide and told us stories. My mom also taught me my artwork. I'm an artist by trade now, and I owe all my thanks to my mom. She taught me to draw, paint, and sculpt. All I surrounded myself with was martial arts and drawing.

In Corpus Christi, we had extended family living in the house, and it was a tumultuous time. I didn't like the strain it put on my mom, so at thirteen years old, I made a solemn promise to God and myself that I would not be a burden to anyone for the rest of my life. And I've kept that promise. My parents are no longer with me in the physical form, but they are with me spiritually.

And every day that I wake up, they are with me; and every night, I say goodnight. I reassure them I'm keeping my promise that I am not a burden to anyone. I've never been drunk, high, or stolen in my entire life. I have been so engulfed with spiritual ways and teachings that there was no room for anything else.

I stuck with martial arts training, and I started training in judo in 1969. I followed that path for seventeen years. Any of the martial arts names that end in "do" mean "the way" and so each martial art has a spiritual aspect of it. Judo means the "gentle way." Each art is not just to hurt or kill, but it teaches you how to stop a fight before it starts — you talk your way out of a fight. When I was around thirty, I started training in aikido. The name aikido means the "way of harmonious spirit or spiritual awakening." Aikido has a genuine concern for the well-being of the attacker. My training in aikido opened up my heart and soul to the spirit world. During my aikido journey, I heard of a Native American black belt aikido follower. People recognized him as a holy man from the start of his practice of aikido. I thought that the combination of "holy man" and aikido practice was an awesome concept, and I looked into that path. As I was seeking people, teachers came into my life to teach me spiritual ways. I studied aikido with Steven Segal, who is also a Buddhist follower. When I started, I knew little about that philosophy. I was in training in California and I felt the similarities between Buddhist and Native teachings. I didn't feel threatened or negative during that training. I made a ten-year commitment to myself that I was going to go on a Buddhist quest and learn everything I could within this ten-year time. During that journey, I was in the presence of many spiritual masters, and it made my heart open up even more. At thirty-two, my spiritual path hit me full throttle, and I surrendered to it. I studied with many holy men in different countries and went to reservations to study with powerful Native medicine men and women. I met people who their people praised, honored, and loved, and I learned from them. My discipline in martial arts made it easy to learn. All this is part of who I am and how I live my life. The discipline of martial arts and being spiritual within the martial arts made it easier to bleed it into the ways of the Native culture and opened more doors for me than I could have ever imagined.

How I Became a Spokesman for Native American Issues in Corpus Christi, Texas

I remember hearing about a gentleman named William Red Fox Humes when I was a child. William Red Fox was a well-known spokesman for Native people and a Sioux Indian rights advocate. He lived in Corpus Christi and traveled all around Texas doing teachings and speaking to groups about the poor treatment of Native Americans by the US government. I remember growing up and thinking I would like to emulate him and how people remembered him. In March 1976, he passed away to the spirit world at ninety-one, and we did a "spirit release" ceremony at his gravesite in Rose Hill Cemetery in Corpus Christi. When I retired from the worldly work (barbering and martial arts), I dedicated the rest of my life to my culture, my people, and my art. To dedicate myself to my culture was to go out and talk publicly in schools, universities, and gatherings of social clubs about the history of our people and our ancestry, to educate about the wrongdoings toward Native people. From those early speaking engagements, my work has escalated to an enormous amount of teachings. I've taken on the task because the truth needs to be told. I tell the history teachers who invite me to speak to be careful what they invite me for because I will tell them the truth. The ones who won the battles, not the misfortunate ones who lost, write everything that students have learned about the history of our people. When the victors write the history, they do so in a way that justifies the way they treated Native Americans. Many people pull me in all these directions for teachings, lessons, and guidance on the right path, and I do what I can for them.

To dedicate myself to my people was to make a concrete and permanent achievement for them. I knew an Elder that once lived in Corpus Christi. He had gathered up the remnants of seven Native American bodies in a shoebox. They were in parts and pieces, and he wanted to rebury them properly in the nearby town of Rockport. I was invited to come and assist him in the reburial. He was the one who saw something in me and said I needed to be on a holy and sacred path. He showed me how to do a reburial for repatriating our ancestors and we talked about all the wrongdoings and he encouraged me to learn more ceremonies.

We dug a hole and buried the remains in a sacred way. From that day on, he told me I should always fight for the Indian burial rights, so I looked into it and researched it.

We became aware that the neighborhood around Ennis Joslin road in Corpus Christi was built on the second largest Native American burial ground in the state of Texas. Workers called me in 1994 to say that they pulled out a small Comanche girl from a site where they were expanding the street. They were going to pave the area over her, and they had removed the bones. The Caller Times newspaper requested that I investigate it, and I felt saddened and performed a ceremony at that specific site. The state had pulled the bones out, and they wouldn't give me the bones to rebury. I started looking into the treatment of burial sites in Corpus Christi and found out that there is much more to it. State workers promptly buried the remains of white settlers, but they sent the remains of Native Americans to archeology labs for study. I learned of a law signed by President Bush in 1990 called the Native American Graves Protection and Repatriation Act (NAGPRA), which gives us rights to reclaim our people and to rebury them properly. Later, I heard a man named Larry Echo Hawk (former Department of Interior's assistant secretary for Indian affairs) speak in Colorado. Going to those meetings in Denver, Colorado, and also in Austin, Texas, was eye-opening. In Austin, I met a maritime archeologist and historical anthropologist named Dr. Fred L. McGhee. Dr. McGhee is the one who really helped me get on the path to repatriating Native American bones. I felt moved to raise awareness about the burial site in Corpus Christi for my people. At first I wanted to rename the street of Ennis Joslin to Sacred Trail. I gave the city $500 to start the paperwork and went door to door with a petition collecting signatures to change the name. The long and short of it is the city didn't change the name, and they kept the five hundred bucks. Then I thought, if I couldn't change the name, I would arrange for the building of a monument on city land at the sacred site. The monument would pay tribute to the ancestors and commemorate the people who have been pulled out of there. It is an ongoing struggle, especially with the present economy, but I'm hoping within my lifetime I can see this monument go up.

The Journey of Pamela Two Spirits Reader

I grew up in a stressful, dysfunctional, and abusive family. I lived in fear of my father and learned to keep my mouth shut. I remember a particular time that I did speak up when my father was beating my younger brother behind closed doors. I begged him to hit me instead. My brother and I were close, and I wonder what would have happened to the family if he had lived. At 16, my only sibling, Kevin, died in a car accident rushing home from a party. That brought more disfunction, and I decided to leave the house by the advice of one of my counselors, who was concerned for my safety. I avoid discussing that period of my childhood with others, except with counselors. I find that it doesn't bring anyone comfort, and ultimately, it doesn't alter the events that occurred. Like all of us, my parents have their own issues and life lessons, and my hope is that they found peace. I'm sorry for what their hearts endured and forgiveness on my part happened years ago. However, I did have residual blockages. For many years, I felt I wasn't good enough, and I mirrored that feeling in my waking life. It was a long time before I finally realized it was a false narrative that I needed to let go of. I still struggle with that particular blockage. We will talk about releasing blockages in a later chapter, because it is such an important teaching. We all deserve to reclaim who we really are.

My childhood wasn't all bad. I was fortunate enough to have loving grandparents. They were positive and loving role models and I stayed at their house as much as possible and most summers. My grandfather took me fishing every Sunday. He was a gentle and quiet man, and I was at peace being in the present moment with him in nature. My grandmother was the opposite personality — she was full of effervescent energy. My grandmother taught me we were all connected by her everyday actions. She loved all people. She had friends who were black, white, brown, rich and poor — she loved them all! My grandmother died when I was thirteen and my grandfather died a few years later of a broken heart. Three years after my grandfather's passing, my brother died in a car accident. The situation left me feeling alone and abandoned. I had no one.

My visions began when I was approximately five years old when a wolf entered my bedroom while I was lying in bed. The wolf positioned himself in the corner, attentively watching over me. Even though it was an enormous wolf, it didn't frighten me. I was confused at first, but then found comfort by the wolf and even felt protected by his watchful eye. He kept looking from side to side and I finally went to sleep feeling safe. Much later, I realized that he was my spirit animal, sent to protect and watch over me. I've experienced recurring visions and dreams of the wolf for many years. In fact, in one dream, I actually transformed into a wolf to protect a woman from a man that was attacking her. I have experienced many types of dreams and visions that have deeply impacted me, and I will weave some of them in my aha moments.

I continued having ceremonial dreams for approximately 30 years, with a Native American spirit guide named Clap Dance. Clap Dance put me through many ceremonies, which made me explore more of the Native ways. I couldn't find a person in history named Clap Dance, but I continued to experience these ceremonial dreams and intuitive spiritual messages from him. One dream in particular pointed me toward becoming a hospice nurse. I finished my commitment to the Air Force as an Air Force Nurse and was a Director of Nursing at a nursing home. The dream, as always, was vivid. In this dream, I was dead. Clap Dance, my Spirit Guide, was in the background drumming in some sort of ceremony and I turned to him and asked, "Am I dead?" He said no, he just wanted me to experience death. It wasn't like anything I read about, like crystal cathedrals or tunnels. I just kept floating up in the sky and suddenly I was flying faster and faster past different topography—from mountains, rivers, grasslands...faster and faster. Then, I could be in any place just by thinking about it. After that dream, I wondered why I even experienced death, but spirit is never wrong. Just based solely on that dream, I became a hospice nurse, which I would have never considered otherwise. Being a hospice nurse and counselor was the most life altering profession I've ever had. Being at the bedside of those transitioning was an honor, and I learned many lessons from my patients. The hospice patients told me about their dreams and visions they were having, which confirmed my own dreams and visions. There was an intuitive knowing and a true spiritual connection with them. It was the feeling of being home, understanding their experience of being simultaneously in the physical and spiritual world. I finally understood completely, without a doubt, that we are all spirits having this human experience. I realized that someday I will also be home again.

I had another ceremonial dream with Clap Dance that led me to a healing program I produced approximately 10 years after the dream. Clap dance was drumming and asked if I wanted to journey. Of course I said yes. At that moment, I underwent a transformation and became a drop of water. Not just a drop of water, but a molecule in a drop of water. I saw myself being the drop of water traveling with the entire body of water. I was content moving along with the water feeling independent, but also with my relations, the water. When we reached the top of a cliff, we all moved down and became part of a waterfall. As I was cascading down, I burst open from my drop and became the entire body of water. It was a feeling of being a separate molecule with water, and then being interconnected with the entire waterfall. I still had my identity, but I was part of everybody else. I then transformed from the waterfall into a molecule of wind traveling with the wind. It was the same feeling as being a separate wind molecule, yet feeling part of my relatives, the wind. Again, I experienced the shifting from my own particle to the "entire" wind. It was such an amazing feeling of interconnectedness. Next, I was a photon in a sunbeam and then the entire sunbeam. What I felt was indescribable, but again, it brought forth understand the dichotomy of being separate, yet understanding that we are all interconnected. I continued to have many ceremonial dreams of interconnectedness with Clap Dance. I was confused about why, but soon realized this was a central teaching of the Red Road. I am convicted in my belief that we, in partnership with Creator, can help heal our body, mind, and spirit. During the isolation of the COVID-19 pandemic in 2020, I attempted to recreate the experience and shared it on YouTube. It was my way of staying connected with others and spread healing during the difficult times. You can find the hypnotherapy program on YouTube or by googling Pamela Two Spirits Reader, Loving Energy.

My visions continued into adulthood. One vision happened with the birth of my son, Jacob. As I was giving birth and after my son came out of the birthing canal, I saw a white light that connected to all people. It was an ethereal light that webbed out of me as I watched it leave the hospital and merge with people on the streets. As it did, I felt a strong sense of interconnectedness with everyone as this light continued to ebb out and expand. I truly felt connected to Creator and all of creation. I'm so grateful for my dreams and experiences with spirit.

For many years, I lived in the Coconino National Forest near Flagstaff, Arizona. We lived off the grid, and I enjoyed walking amongst the trees, listening to the elk, eagles, and the wind. Sometimes I took off my shoes, and walked barefoot in the footprints of the elk, feeling their energy. I found solace sitting with my relations, and I owe most of my healing to nature. My life continues to be diverse, but there has always been one common thread—the understanding that we are all related. The indigenous cultures have a deep knowing of this wisdom ingrained in their hearts.

Larry Running Turtle and I met at an art festival in Texas approximately 20 years ago. We realized there was a commonality between us and we had similar philosophies. Of course, it was a synchronistic meeting, which is another chapter in this book. Larry was interested in a particular dream I had about the star people. In my dream, I met Clap Dance and asked him for an answer about all the ceremonies he put me through. Clap Dance told me to ask the woman behind the tree. I looked and saw a Native American woman by a large tree. When I reached her, she beckoned me to actually go into the tree, and I did. We looked down, and I saw myself dancing on a platform in a Native way. As I danced, I was pulling stars out of the sky and was putting them back in a unique pattern. The Native American woman said that she just wanted me to see who I was. I feel like I have finally understood her message. My heart has always been leading and beckoning me to continue walking the Good Red Road and encouraging others to do the same. Like Larry, our lives have had many diverse lessons, but there has been one common thread we both have: the sacredness of all creation.

I believe everyone must live their truth, which they innately know if they listen. One of the greatest teachings I received was from a Buddhist monk who once told me that whatever path you're on, if it is a path that leads to love and light, then it is a good path. I hold that teaching close to my heart. I realize that loving words and acts of kindness, no matter how large or small, have a vibrational energy that heals us. Whatever path we are on, we can be of loving service to ourselves and others. It is about loving and honoring yourself, your brothers and sisters, and revering all life. It is about making each day count spiritually. It's about making every encounter a heartfelt one.

GATHERING OUR SPIRITUAL MEDICINES

What have we done as inhabitants of the earth? How can we look around and not see the disrespect we've caused Mother Earth? There are consequences to our actions. It is time to repair the damage to her and to our brothers and sisters. Great spiritual teachers have brought us many lessons, medicine, and healing, yet we still have wars and conflicts. Mother Earth suffers now more than ever, as do her children. When will we understand that every single thing--from the drop of water we drink to the stars in the sky—is sacred? When will we understand we must take care of our brothers and sisters? Can we find the commonality of everything around us rather than focus on things that divide us? We all came here with original instructions from our ancestors. These teachings interweave into the fabric of our being for all people, even though some religions and other institutional entities try to ignore or discount this fact. We must remember our greatest original instruction—we are all interconnected.

The Hopi Creed informs us that if we do not establish a spiritual connection with Mother Earth and cannot comprehend the spiritual essence of life on earth, the likelihood of our survival is low. Plain and simple. Frank Walters wrote a Book of the Hopi in 1963, revealing the Prophecy to the world. The Hopi Prophecy is an ancient story about Earth's past great apocalyptic cycles, with instructions on how to avoid a fourth destruction. According to the prophecy, the earth has undergone three destructions created by humankind turning their collective back on Mother Earth and allowing greed to rule their actions. Our current world (the 4th) is on the brink of self-destruction, and the only way to avoid destruction is for humankind to reconnect with their spiritual nature and become responsible stewards of the earth. If humankind cannot do this, then this world's end is inevitable. There are nine signs the fourth world is coming to an end, according to the Hopi Prophecy. Many people believe all signs have come to pass except the last prophecy. No one knows when the last prophecy will happen, but it's obvious we need to pay attention to what we are doing to Mother Earth.

One example is deforestation and climate change. Did you know that over half of all plant and animal species in the world call rainforests their home? Do you also know they are crying to be saved? The Rainforest Foundation provides this sobering fact in 2020. "The current rate of destruction is about 1 acre each second, which is a bit less than a US football field. Expanded, that amounts to 60 acres/min, 3,600/hour, 86,400/day, 2.6 million/month, and 31.5 million acres." We are failing our Mother.

Instead of writing about all the destruction we have done and continue to do, we want to inspire and encourage our readers to gather their spiritual medicines to empower you on your spiritual journey. Many people are realizing the need to gather teachings from Native People, and if you open your heart, teachers will appear. There are so many teachings, medicines, and information available for us to gather. For example, different tribes have plant medicine from the plant people that may or may not be hidden. Some Native Americans are protective of these medicines and might not be so open to share. You have to understand, everything has been taken from them, so they sometimes find it difficult to trust. For example, in Arizona, poaching has caused the white sage to be dwarfed in size. If it continues to go much longer, white sage will cease to exist and will throw off the balance of nature. Therefore, it is so vital to come back to Indigenous teachings of respecting the plant medicine, and not taking more than you need. Native

Americans are open to teaching and showing you if your heart is open to the spirit of the medicine, and not using the knowledge or plant for greed.

When you gather spiritual medicines, you can do so physically, mentally, and emotionally. Every thing has spirit medicine. Take, for example, a bear product — such as a claw, rug, hat or hide. When you adorn or own it, you now take on the spiritual medicine of the bear. Some people even consider you a spiritual person because they honor the bear medicine. If Native people feel sick and they don't have the medicine to take, they can get bear medicine and pray with it and hold it close to their heart. They think of the journey the bear took from birth to death to be here with them, and honor the sacred medicines they ate to exist before it came to them. There are examples where people wearing a big bear claw necklace, and others ask to honor it or take the spirit on. If you say yes, they hold their hands as if they are going to drink water, but they get a hand full of air from the claws to their mouth and do that 4 times, and by doing that, they take part of the spirit of the bear.

There are times you may need the spirit of the turtle to withdraw and go in your shell and you think about how that sacred animal protects itself. When you do so, you remember the lesson of the turtle. There are sacred animals, plants and stones that all have certain spiritual medicines that you can use. If you are in the hospital, they may take your medicines, but you can go into a meditative state of mind and remember your spirit animal, be with that animal, and ask for that medicine. You can ask the spirit guides of that animal how they would cure themselves and take that journey in your mind. How would the hummingbird heal themselves, or the butterfly, and you metaphorically think about that. Even people in prison can still engage in ceremony without the pipe, even if they are stripped of everything. They can do their songs without their drums. We have evolved into a society that places high value on material possessions for our ceremonies, when in reality, they are not necessary for their success. Ceremonies can be created in your mind. You also have the ability to choose any animal as your spirit animal, and it's ultimately up to you to determine which animal resonates most with you. One method for discovering your spirit animal is to center yourself and pay attention to the animal that naturally gravitates toward you, or the animal that you feel drawn to. You might have dreams about a particular animal and then encounter it in nature. Seeing an animal repeatedly in dreams, visions, or encounters in the physical world can be seen as a way that the animal is trying to communicate with you and guide you towards a deeper connection with its energy and wisdom. Perhaps you have a collection of a particular animal around your house, or you're reading about a particular animal that you find fascinating? Maybe you are drawn to the strength or quality of a particular animal? Stay close to your spirit animal and hear their lessons, teachings, and embrace their healings.

There are major evolutionary events happening now on Mother Earth and we need to take the journey with honor and not fear and learn as much as we can about our medicines. Plants, rocks, minerals, water, air, and even the dirt we walk on are spiritual medicines. Water was the first medicine given to our planet. Stop and think about your body. It is approximately 60% water. To stay healthy, we need to drink clean and pure water. Water is sacred to the Native people, air is sacred, plant and animals are sacred and Native people have always understood this. They know, feel, and understand the truth of having an interconnected relationship with everything around them.

Do you know we have similar shaped DNA molecules with the plant and tree people? And that the plant people feel pain and experience emotions? They even have a network of communication and feed each other if needed. Think about a tree. The tree provides its branches in order for us to have shelter. They make pipes, drums, and sweat lodges for ceremonies. They make paper, furniture, floors, and really just about anything you can imagine. Their logs provide fire that keeps us warm and to cook our food. Even the flames are alive with spiritual medicine. The smoke carries messages up to creator, so prayers can be heard. Trees provide our oxygen and remove harmful gases like carbon dioxide. It's time to get close to these things, make your journeys, visit the sacred sites if you can. We need to understand that even the ocean has a language we can hear if we silence our minds. There is a voice in the rivers, the leaves, the grass, the wind, the star people; everything. One of our important spiritual medicine is to quiet our minds, listen with our hearts, and take these lessons into our form. Join us and delve deeper into these spiritual teachings.

Aha Moments

Throughout the book, we will refer to Larry or Pam's Aha Moments. Aha moments are personal recollections, asides, and accounts of events that illuminate the topic discussed in that chapter.

Larry's Aha Moment

I help out at a crystal shop and people ask me many questions and I give as many teachings as I can. They will ask, am I going to find God in this particular rock/crystal? Of course, lift a rock; Creator is there. Cut wood, Creator will be there. The Great Spirit is in the space in-between. Even in the clouds. I was driving to the doctor for the first time in San Antonio for an important procedure. I looked out the car window and there was a cross above the cloud. There's Creator right there. Our spiritual medicines include listening to the silent people, which is one of many lessons you will learn in this book.

Pam's Aha Moment

We were picnicking with two of my son's city friends in the forest near our cabin deep in the woods. I noticed the two young boys giggling and throwing rocks at a lizard, so I walked over and explained respect, one lesson of the Good Red Road. We explored the forest and stopped to hug an enormous pine tree. We breathed in its vanilla scent and thanked the tree for being an important teacher. I pointed out a grandfather tree that overlooked the younger ones. We took in one important lesson of the plant people — the importance of spreading love and kindness. Nature is such a wonderful place to feel Creator's love and to gather our spiritual medicines.

What is life? It is the flash of a firefly in the night. It is the breath of a buffalo in the wintertime. It is the little shadow which runs across the grass and loses itself in the sunset.

— Blackfoot

THE RED

ROAD

The old Lakota was wise. He knew that a man's heart, away from nature, becomes hard. He knew that lack of respect for growing living things soon led to lack of respect for humans, too. So he kept his children close to nature's softening influence.

— Luther Standing Bear

During the time of creation, creator imbued all races with original instructions on how to live with Mother Earth and with each other. Over time, many of us have lost our original instructions, although many Native people have held onto theirs. These instructions apply to all mankind, not just one nation. They might be simple, but they can take a lifetime to understand. We hope the time has come where all nations are awakening to the fact that wars, conflict, hate, and division are not the answers. There is a yearning for the guiding light of indigenous leadership and wisdom because it is rooted in the respect and interconnectedness of all life. It's time to come together and take responsibility to respect and love one another. We must gather our spiritual medicines so we can heal little by little. This includes honoring Great Spirit, the two-legged, four-legged, the ones that fly, swim, crawl — along with the rocks, minerals, four winds and four seasons, Father Sky, Mother Earth and everything in-between. This brings us to the teachings of the Red Road. The Red Road is a lifelong journey of understanding how to live your life on the right path, and it is the crux of our spiritual medicine.

The phrase The Good Road or Red Road is a term used by many Native American tribal communities to represent one who is walking the road of balance, living right and following the rules of Creator. The Red Road is a behavior, attitude, a way of living and doing with reverence, of walking

strong yet softly, so as not to harm or disturb other life — John Redtail Freesoul (Cheyenne-Arapahoe), Spokesman for the Redtail Hawk Medicine Society, from his book *Breath of the Invisible*1

Walking The Red Road signifies a deep commitment to living with an intrinsic respect for yourself, others, and all creation. It is living in love, gratitude, and evolving in sacred ways. Tribal leaders following the teachings of the Red Road died defending not only their land, but protecting these principles and their ceremonies. Ceremonies were the very core of tribal strength, renewal, and connection — it was part of their very being, but ceremonies were banned because they were not considered the "correct way" of worship. To be blunt, colonizers looked down upon Native people as savages and forced them to perform their ceremonies in secret. Imagine dying for your principles. That's what happened to many great Native leaders. The Religious Crimes Code of 1883 banned Native dances and ceremonies. This Code gave authority to use force and imprisonment to stop cultural practices they deemed immoral or subversive to federal government mandated assimilation policies. They finally repealed the Code in the 1970s. Restrictive codes are part of the methods the U.S. employed to restrict the cultural identity of American Indian tribes. Let us emphasize and rephrase: authorities imprisoned or killed many political, cultural, and spiritual leaders just for living their way of life.

The following are the Native American Indian Traditional Code of Ethics printed in 1984 in by the Four Worlds Development project. In October 1994, the "Inter-Tribal Times" adapted and reprinted it.

Native American Code of Ethics by the United Cherokee of Indian

    I.   Days Blessing. Each morning upon rising, and each evening before sleeping, give thanks for the life within you and for all life, for the good things the Creator has given you, and for the opportunity to grow a little more each day. Consider your thoughts and actions of the past day and seek for the courage and strength to be a better person. Seek for the things that will benefit others.

II. Respect. Respect means to feel or show honor or esteem for someone or something, to consider the well-being of, or to treat someone or something with deference or courtesy. Showing respect is a basic law of life. Treat every person from the tiniest child to the oldest elder with respect at all times.

    A. Special respect should be given to elders, parents, teachers, and community leaders.

    B. No person should be made to feel put down by you; avoid hurting other hearts as you would avoid a deadly poison.

    C. Touch nothing that belongs to someone else (especially sacred objects) without permission, or an understanding between you.

    D. Respect the privacy of every person; never intrude on a person's quiet moment or personal space.

    E. Never walk between people who are conversing.

    F. Never interrupt people who are conversing.

    G. Speak in a soft voice, especially when you are in the presence of elders, strangers, or others to whom special respect is due.

    H. Do not speak unless invited to do so at gatherings where elders are present (except to ask what is expected of you, should you be in doubt)

    I. Never speak about others in a negative way, whether they are present or not.

    J. Treat the earth and all of her aspects as your mother.

Show deep respect for the mineral world, the plant world, and the animal world. Do nothing to pollute our Mother; rise up with wisdom to defend her.

K. Show deep respect for the beliefs and religion of others.

L. Listen with courtesy to what others say, even if you feel that what they are saying is worthless. Listen with your heart.

M. Respect the wisdom of the people in the council. Once you give an idea to a council meeting, it no longer belongs to you. It belongs to the people. Respect demands that you listen to the ideas of others in the council and that you do not insist that your idea prevails. Indeed, you should freely support the ideas of others if they are true and good, even if those ideas are quite different from the ones you have contributed. The clash of ideas brings forth the Spark of Truth.

III. Once a council has decided something in unity, respect demands that no one speak secretly against what has been decided. If the council has made an error, that error will become apparent to everyone in its own time.

IV. Be truthful at all times, and under all conditions.

V. Always treat your guests with honor and consideration. Give your best food, your best blankets, the best part of your house, and your best service to your guests.

VI. The hurt of one is the hurt of all, the honor of one is the honor of all.

VII. Receive strangers and outsiders with a loving heart as members of the human family.

VIII. All the races and tribes in the world are like the different colored flowers of one meadow. All are beautiful. As children of the Creator, they must all be respected.

IX. To serve others, to be of some use to family, community, nation, and the world is one of the main purposes for which human beings have been created. Do not fill yourself with your own affairs and forget your most important tasks. True happiness comes only to those who dedicate their lives to the service of others.

X. Observe moderation and balance in all things.

XI. Know those things that lead to your well-being, and those things that lead to your destruction.

XII. Listen to and follow the guidance given to your heart. Expect guidance to come in many forms-in prayer, in dreams, in times of quiet solitude, and in the words and deeds of wise elders and friends.

Black Elk spoke of all the people on the Red Road as being one interconnected circle of people that made a sacred hoop. He believed only you can walk your journey, but many are on the road. When you are on the Good Red Road, you live your life in such a way that you are in harmony with the world around you.

To achieve harmony with the world, you must first incorporate healthy self-esteem into your form, which is respecting yourself, respecting others, and respecting all things. Respect is one of the basic principles of The Red Road. It is easy to lose your way by not applying the principles of self-esteem. When you don't have good self-esteem, you may follow the wrong crowd or live your life according to others' values instead of living an authentic life. Think back to your parents or your role models. How did they show and incorporated self-esteem into their daily life? How did you learn to respect yourself? Are you honoring yourself by promoting self-care? Or are you dishonoring yourself by taking on more than you can handle, overeating, drinking or smok-

ing to excess, saying yes when you mean no? If you grew up being neglected, abused, or in an environment that didn't nurture your well-being, it might be hard to even grasp how to love yourself. When you
don't feel worthy, how can you be kind to yourself? We want you to understand that you are worthy and you can build a positive frame-work
for your life. You cannot love and respect another person or Mother
Earth when you don't nurture, respect, or love yourself. When you nurture yourself, your inner light becomes stronger, and soon you are like
a lighthouse, beaming your loving light out to others. If you don't feel
worthy, there could be obstacles to overcome. We'll discuss this further
in a later chapter. Releasing blockages is an important concept to grasp
in order to heal and bring more love and light into your life. We will
discuss our personal blockages in our aha moments that took years to
release. We are all trying to navigate the Red Road with our blockages,
warts, and all life has to throw at us. So you see, you are not alone; the
same proponents of life run through all our veins and we all bleed red
no matter who or what we are. As we talked about in the previous chapter, we all have Creator's love that abides in us. We have a spiritual mission to fulfill our soul's purpose, as we are divinely created. Our purpose
and journey is to accept we are love, and then we can emulate love.

When we dishonor and disregard another person, belittle them,
laugh at them, gossip, or direct anger toward them, that is not walking
a good road. When the intent is to hurt your brothers and sisters, it
doesn't align with walking the Good Red Road. The next time you say
an unkind word to your brother or sister, or another person directs
anger toward you, know this is not true to the teachings. Before you
say or do anything, ask yourself if what you are saying is true, kind, and
gentle. This is when you become mindful of your speech. When you
disregard and become apathetic and disrespectful to your surroundings, that also leads you away from the Red Road. For example, when
people toss their garbage or pollute our waters and the air we breathe,

they don't show the teachings of the Good Red Road. When we dishonor anything, including the four-legged or winged ones, that further turns us away from the Red Road teachings.

When we walk the Good Red Road, we don't judge our brothers and sisters — no matter what. Being nonjudgmental is such a big lesson. We all have different spiritual lessons to learn, and one person's life lesson is not another person's life lesson. Not everyone is going to do what you think they should do. In fact, it is not about you. Every human being is on their own spiritual path. We are all here to learn, no matter who you are. It doesn't mean you join your loved ones knee-deep in their drama. It means hear them, but don't get entrapped in their pity. You can listen and be the mirror if they choose to see. You can't force your solutions on to others' problems. Ram Dass, a spiritual leader and author, says that you have no right to take away someone's suffering because not only does it alienate them, but you don't understand why they are suffering. Maybe they choose to be a victim, or maybe this is their soul's journey? From a different perspective, what you see as a problem may not be an issue to that person.

Understand that we have a part of the Great Spirit with us at all times. How can we judge others or judge ourselves if we are part of Creator? How can we consider ourselves complete failures if we are made in love? We are not here to focus on our mistakes, but to learn from them. If you don't learn from your mistakes, then what was the point? Instead of focusing on your mistakes, question your intent. If your intent was good, there is no such thing as a failure, it's just a learning experience. Focus on the progress you are making, rather than getting caught up in the challenges of the lesson, as this shift in perspective will bring you peace. It's important to stay true to your values and keep moving forward with positivity and determination. Trust that everything will work out in the end, even if it doesn't look that way in the moment. Remember, it's all about the journey and the growth that comes from it.

The common denominator of any spiritual life and/or religion is to love, honor, and respect all things. The Red Road is no different. It is a way of life. If you can keep these key principles in your daily life, you are well on your way to walking the Good Red Road and gathering your spiritual medicines. Find your place in the world. Perhaps up to now, you are not practicing walking The Good Red Road. Okay, but today is a new day. Why can't you do so today? How can you take action in this moment to rejuvenate your spirit, strengthen your relationships, and shift your thinking positively to align with the Red Road teachings? What small steps can you take? Perhaps you can choose to stop putting junk in your body, junk in your mind, junk in your soul? Maybe you can stop drinking or stop polluting or recycle? What small lessons can you bring into your form that will help you respect and honor yourself and others? Where do you want to see your life? Maybe you took one step back, but don't forget the three steps forward. We can all improve, but don't lose sight of the good things you are doing right now! The bottom line is we are not perfect, but just knowing where we need to put our attention or where we are off balance can help on our path. Review the Red Road principles daily, and try to incorporate them into your life.

To summarize, whatever point you are in your life, be kind and respect yourself and your brothers and sisters. Take care of Mother Earth and her children along your journey and don't give up on that commitment. Love, honor, and respect all things. We are here to learn many lessons, and we understand there are times in our lives when we will, or have, hit despair, depression or just struggle through some issues. And then there are other times when life seems to go our way, when the sky opens up and shines as bright as the sun. These events are part of our journey everyone visits. As you navigate this book, you will gain more empowering practices for your Red Road journey.

Larry's Aha Moment

There are a lot of Native people who were not raised in the Native ways. They might have been adopted or born in a suburban world without elders teaching them the ways. But now, some have it in their heart to learn the Native ways. I have people ask me about teachings on the sacred ways. They want to enrich their ways on how to get reconnected to Mother Earth herself, so I tell them to join a drum circle, seek teachers and ask questions about how to get on the Red Road. Research Native ways by reading books or articles. Getting on the Red Road means you are now going to accept these sacred ways of our ancestors and of our people. It means being able to honor Mother Earth and her children and not be disrespectful to them, but to put respect back into everything. It is accepting all knowledge as it comes in, no matter what nation it came from. No longer do we study just one particular nation. Everybody studies a variation of nations because it is not a matter of nations, it is a matter of going back to our original instructions. We had no separation back then. When the white culture came, it put separation into our culture and all of us. We lost that respect toward one another and how to live with one another, but it's all coming back, regaining full circle now. We are connecting as a community by gathering groups of individuals to embody the teachings of our ancestors. Students are seeking guidance from elders to learn and one day carry on the teachings themselves. There are people coming forth to learn more and more of the sacred ways, so these ways cannot be lost. We teach the pipe to as many people who want to learn the pipe, for that is one of our most important teachings that we have. We teach our songs, our Native way of praying, and our Native ways of how to preserve life. This is all about how to stay on the Red Road. I am awakened to this daily with the many people who come to me and ask for teachings, prayers, or ceremonies.

Pam's Aha Moment

One Red Road lesson that has stuck with me for many years is the time I went to a Buddhist monastery for 7 days to study meditation. I arrived at the temple full of joy and excited to begin my journey. It was a long trip, and I needed to use the restroom right away. Before I ran off to the bathroom, someone handed me a sheet of paper that stated a few rules to abide by during my stay. I took the rules of the temple that the monk gave me, and I read them while I sat on the toilet. Rule number one was, "Do not kill." What an easy one, I thought. I've killed no one, never had the desire to kill anyone, nor did I ever plan on killing anyone. Got it! These rules are easy breezy! Just as I finished that thought, a spider came running across the floor toward me, and without giving it another thought, I stepped on it and squashed it. I then looked up from my instruction sheet and looked around the stall. I saw all these cobwebs with spiders in them, all eyes staring at me. Oh crap, in more ways than one, I realized I had just broken rule number one while sitting on the toilet within the first minute of arriving at the temple. I was so smug that I thought the rules they had given me only applied to human-to-human interaction. No, the monks meant what they said: "Do not kill — anything!" My intent wasn't dishonorable, but in my thoughtless haste, I had decided that the commitment to an instruction only applied to a fraction of the world and not the whole. From that day forth, I try to respect all things, including spiders.

Another example I'd like to share occurred when I was a nurse in the Air Force. I had a patient who was a Jehovah's Witness. I knew little about that religion, and I was a young nurse just out of school. My patient and I bonded during her admission, and she trusted me. Her blood work came in, and it showed that she needed blood. It wasn't an emergency, but getting some blood would make her recovery a lot faster and easier. She was filled with doubt and uncertainty, torn between her religious beliefs and the well-being of her children, but she trusted me and received the blood. Years later, I learned that certain diseases were not tested for in the blood during that timeframe. I talked her into doing something that she wasn't comfortable doing and was contrary to her beliefs. Who was I to think I knew what better served her? The experience was a big lesson for me.

TO ALL OUR RELATIONS

H*ear me, four quarters of the world—a relative I am! Give me the strength to walk the soft earth, a relative to all that is! Give me the eyes to see and the strength to understand that I may be like you. With your power, only can I face the winds.*

Great Spirit, Great Spirit, my Grandfather, all over the earth the faces of living things are all alike. With tenderness have these come up out of the ground. Look upon these faces of children without number and with children in their arms, that they may face the wind and walk the good road to the day of quiet.

This is my prayer, hear me! — "Black Elk's Prayer for All Life"

The more knowledge we acquire, the more mystery we find... A human being is part of the whole, called by us the Universe, a part limited in time and space. He experienced himself, his thoughts and feelings, as something separate from the rest—a kind of optical illusion of his consciousness. The delusion is a kind of prison for us, restricting us to our personal desires and to affection for a few persons nearest to us. Our task must be to free ourselves from this prison by widening our circle of compassion to embrace all living creatures and the whole of nature in its beauty.

— Albert Einstein

Alan Watts, author speaker and philosopher, states, "Each of the 20 books I have had published carries at the same destination from a different point of departure, as the spokes of a wheel converge at the same hub from different points on the rim. Taking the presumes of Christian dogmatics, Hindu mythology, Buddhist psychology, Zen practice, psychoanalysis, behaviorism, or logical positivism, I have tried to show that all are aiming, however disputatiously at one center."2

Look deep within you, and know you are not separate from those around you. We are all connected to each other on a deep, spiritual level, as we are all part of the same divine tapestry of existence. The same particles, DNA, molecular structure, and spirit that make us human, resides in all of us. When we separate ourselves by race, creed, economic status, or anything else for that matter, we pull away from sacredness. When we put our focus on how different we are from one another, we become divided. By shifting our focus to what we have in common versus what divides us, we realize one of our spiritual medicines — we are all connected. Don't let people, organizations, or religions that try to divide us deceive you. That makes us weak and vulnerable. Ego divides and categorizes for power and control. Do not allow yourself to be deceived by these ways. The growing division in our world serves as a poignant reminder of the urgent need to embrace unity and acknowledge the spiritual bond that unites us all. We must rise above these divisions and recognize that at our core, we are all one. Differences of opinions or perspectives are normal. Anger, fear and hurting our brothers and sisters are not. We must see this division for what it is — an illusion.

When someone talks about division or how bad one side is or the other, simply state we must learn to get along. Lead by example and illuminate the path forward through your actions. You don't need to match the energies or argue the point. Like a radio, turn to another station or deflect by changing the subject. Some of you might be thinking — but you don't know my family! Well, if you tell them you feel uncomfortable and you want to talk about anything else and if they don't honor your feelings, you can take a walk or just not respond. Why lower your vibration or dishonor yourself by subjecting yourself to that energy?

Our society is in a constant state of defining ourselves. We use labels, societal norms and expectations to create identity. The process of defining ourselves can create divisions between individuals who identify with different labels or groups, leading to conflict or discrimination. Ego's need to label and define every aspect of our lives often serves to further divide us. By placing labels and judgments on ourselves and others, we create barriers between us. This can manifest in conflicts based on perceived differences or feelings of superiority or inferiority. It can limit our ability to truly connect with others on a deeper level when we are focused on external definitions of identity. We may fail to see the common humanity and experiences that unite us. Whether you are a Christian, Muslim, White, Black, or Native American, we are all connected. At one point, Native Americans were not even recognized as human beings. There are countless historical examples of other cultures being abused, gassed, killed, and even annihilated. Wars were fought because of our differences. Conflict and wars continue at this very moment. People continue to commit atrocities to other people and animals around the world. Clearly, many have forgotten that we are all brothers and sisters.

If you harbor anger towards a brother or sister, try embracing the Dalai Lama's teachings on compassion. He said to distinguish between the action and the actor and emphasized the importance of cultivating love, compassion and non-violence. The Dalai Lama's teachings on compassion leads us to feelings of self-confidence and kindness. No matter what your belief, without compassion, you simply can not be happy. He believed in the power of religious traditions to cultivate compassion, yet recognized that a person can be sincere, good-hearted, and wonderful without religious faith.

Christ taught many lessons on compassion. When asked what was the greatest commandment, Jesus responded it was to love God with all our heart, mind and strength. But he added that the second commandment is like the first: "Love your neighbor as yourself" Matthew 22:34-40. Compassion is the first step in bringing about healing in ourselves, families, neighborhoods, communities, cities, countries, and the world. Having a religious ideology doesn't mean you're automatically following principles of acceptable moral and ethical behavior. Religion or no religion, belief or no belief, the choice to practice compassion is your own. Some religious beliefs have been used to justify conflicts and wars throughout history, driven by political and social factors rather than the teachings of compassion and tolerance. No matter our religious ideologies, we must put aside our differences and start talking about the commonality that we share. In doing so, we all heal. We heal ourselves and then vibrationally we start to heal the world. Imagine if we were heroes in our children's eyes by being a role model and spokesperson for compassion? When they look back after we're gone, wouldn't it be awesome knowing they will share stories about how kind we were? What footsteps would you like to leave behind? It's not too late to start.

All teachings, whether they are Native American, Buddhist, Christian or from other outstanding teachers, have one thing in common: love. Learn to care, feed, and clothe the untouchables. When you can do this to all people, you see Creator within you and others. Visit the sick, the elderly; love the unlovables. Try not to hold judgment on anyone, because we all have different life lessons. Remember, their lesson is not your lesson. See through the eyes of the Buddha, Christ, or another great teacher you admire or look up to. Maybe your mother, father, or another person demonstrated to you great compassion. Emulate that person.

This book has one primary message throughout. We are spirits having a human experience, not a human having a spiritual experience. You may have forgotten this, but we want to awaken you. You don't have to seek God; the Great Spirit is everywhere. Look at one another as we are all one relation. As soon as we see each other as separate in any form, we separate ourselves as a whole. When we start judging and labeling, we start separating. Embrace your sacredness as well. Look in the mirror first thing in the morning and look at that awesome sacred being! Perfect? No! We are here to evolve and learn. There will be times you do something you are not proud of. We've all been there, so please stop beating yourself over the head! Honor yourself, no matter what you have done in the past. If you can forgive yourself, you can forgive others. Start to put more and more compassion into your form. Maybe you need to be reminded of your sacredness? Some people set aside a special area inside or outside the house where they go when they need some comfort. Or perhaps there is a special area where you read, meditate, pray, or relax. It's good to have a place in your home where you have some of your special and sacred totems. It may be a picture of a loved one, a candle, a fetish, a cross, sage, crystals, a mantra, or anything you identify with that feels sacred. It's a pleasant reminder that sacredness is all around you. Look out the window or go out in nature. There is nothing quite like nature to connect you to the sacredness of all things. When you get away from the computer, technology, texting, and all the man-made gadgets, you give yourself a moment to connect with sacredness. Animals help us do that daily. Just watch and listen to the animals play and how they go about their daily activities. How can you not feel connected? How can you not smile?

Every part of this earth is sacred to my people. Every shining pine needle, every sandy shore, every mist in the dark woods, every clearing, and every humming insect is holy in the memory and experience of my people. What-

ever befalls the earth befalls the sons of the earth. Man did not weave the web of life; he is merely a strand in it. Whatever he does to the web, he does to himself. — Chief Seattle, 1854

We are part of everything the Great Spirit offers — including the trees, the rocks, the grass, the sky, the wind. Our interconnectedness allows us to receive teachings, healings, and medicine from our surroundings. When a tree breathes out oxygen, you get the much needed oxygen to live. When a tree has fallen, it goes back to the earth or it can make implements that are useful to humans. It can provide housing for the animals in the forest, or it can provide shelter or fire to help us live. When we eat the plant and animal life, they become part of us and nourish our body. When you pray over food, you are giving thanks, as well as bringing in the plant's spirit or animal in a good way, to help heal your body. It's a sacred ceremony.

Even molecules of water can be a loving gift that is bestowed upon us. There is a bestselling book titled *The Hidden Messages in Water* by Dr. Masaru Emoto.3 Dr. Emoto uses high-speed photography to take pictures of frozen water molecules. He found that with positive and loving thoughts, these molecules of water formed beautiful brilliant crystals, whereas negative thought produced asymmetrical, dull, and incomplete crystals. When we pray and give thanks for the food we eat, we are thanking Creator and thanking the plant and animal life. But now there is proof there is another benefit of praying; we are healing our bodies.

Just taking in your breath is very sacred. Our breath is a sacred and interconnected force that binds us all together. Breathing itself is a ceremony that you can perform anywhere. You don't have to make a special trip or run off to Mexico or Peru to find enlightenment. Being aware of our breath is a powerful reminder that we can connect with our sacredness and feel the presence within us. Air is essential to our life force. Imagine if we didn't have clean, healthy air to breathe? By taking slow deep breaths, you activate your body's relaxation response, reducing stress hormones and promoting a sense of calmness. This practice helps to bring awareness to the present moment, allowing you to let go of racing thoughts and emotions. Our breath is indeed a sacred and interwoven connection.

To summarize, it's crucial to recognize our interdependence with all forms of life, and it is now more important than ever to shift towards coexisting harmoniously rather than taking and destroying. Our awareness of the divine within ourselves and in all living beings enables us to see our experiences as integral parts of a larger spiritual path. Indigenous people possess a deep connection to and understanding of the universal language of interconnectedness that exists among all living things. From the drop of water we drink to the stream that flows down the mountain; it is all spirit. From the sky and stars above, to all the leaves that drop from the trees; they all have messages. Somehow, we lost the ability to listen to these messages and forgot how to gather our spiritual medicines. We want you to re-awaken to the fact that we are all related and of one relation.

Larry's Aha Moment

According to one of our creation stories, when the world was made, it was created using nothing but spirit. When the trees were given to us, they consisted entirely of spirit. The plant life we received was solely created from spirit. The two-legged were all created with nothing but spirit. The animals embody the same thing; nothing but spirit. Somehow or another, the two-legged disconnected themselves with spirit and the plant and animal life. We all became separate. Look what we have done to Mother Earth and each other because of this separation.

Before Christ appeared to our people, our ancestors saw everything as interconnected — everything was a blessing bestowed upon us. They took nothing for granted. They held everything in honor and reverence. The first time I felt truly connected to God was back in 1976, when I had surgery on my knee. I remember after surgery hearing bells ringing and people shuffling all around me. I had flatlined and was clinically dead. I saw myself up above looking down at the people working on me in the hospital room, and I had a glimmer of my mom praying in the other room. A substantial change happened to me right then. A perfect peace encompassed me, and I was face to face with Christ himself. That was a big turning point in my life. I started walking in sacredness. I had a second near-death experience six or seven years later. I saw and talked to a lot of my deceased friends and other people who had died. Again, more than ever, it reinforced my decision to walk in sacredness. Lightning struck me while I was sitting on my porch at home in 2019, resulting in yet another near-death experience. I know I am alive for a spiritual reason and everyday I ask the spirit people and creator for guidance to help people understand how sacred they are. I want to give them hope and to help them awaken. I hope my message from my heart reaches out and touches your heart.

My mom taught me many lessons of our original instructions and how to be one with the plant and animal people. I remember when I was around six, I watched my mom catch fish, and then later that day she called me outside and asked to help dig a trench. She put the fish in the trench and then our garden seeds so that the fish become part of the soil to help give the plant life the right nutrients. I felt the aha moment right there because my mom taught me how to grow food to feed our siblings. It made me appreciate life. We should all teach our children how to plant a small garden, even if it is a tomato plant in a container. To plant and grow from Mother Earth is part of Native people's original instructions.

When I am getting ready to eat the plant or animal life, I give thanks to all our relations. As I pray, I say may the spirit of the plant and the spirit of the animal bless and nourish our body as Creator intended. As Native people, we thank the plant and animal life that have sacrificed their lives in order to give us life. When I see something beautiful in front of me, I give thanks to all our relations. No matter what I receive from Mother Earth herself, I give thanks to all my relations. If I meet a new friend that is going to become a lifelong friend, I give thanks within the silence of my breath to all my relations. Even when I meet a new cat, dog, or any animal, I give thanks to all my relations. When I go into any sacred area, I give thanks to all our relations. Native people give thanks to these because we believe we are all connected.

Pam's Aha Moment

I remember the time when I first felt the connection of Creator's love; when I really felt it. During my time in college, I was fortunate to have a remarkable nun as one of my teachers whom I greatly admired and respected. She would assign us the task of meditating on a specific Bible verse and then writing an essay reflecting on our thoughts and insights. I typically wrote essays that met the minimum requirements, but I made an effort on this assignment out of deep respect for her. I meditated and meditated on the verse, but nothing came to me. I kept trying and became increasingly frustrated because I was really trying to do the assignment! All these thoughts kept going through my head like I wasn't worthy of God's love, and he didn't want to talk to me and so on.

I was not feeling God at that point in my life. It was a traumatic time for me. My brother had recently died in a car accident and I felt really, really alone. My life was in turmoil, and I didn't even know why I was even trying. If God loved me, why did he take my brother? Where was God's love? Why was my life such a mess? Perhaps I was a terrible person and God didn't love me the way I was? My parents didn't love me. I was so far removed from the person I thought I needed to be. I stopped trying to meditate, and I turned on my radio, feeling rejected and down on myself. The first words that came from the radio at that exact moment were Billy Joel's *"I Love You Just the Way You Are."* It hit me like a ton of bricks. This immense feeling ran through my body like a shock wave. God loves me just the way I am. No matter what — imperfections and all. At that moment, I truly felt God, and that song still reminds me of His message.

I also vividly remember another experience where I felt a straight connection to Creator. I worked as a hospice nurse and had a scheduled visit with a patient who was actively dying. He was in a coma at the hospital and it was my first time visiting with him. The nurses came up to me and said, "This is a horrible person. His family won't even visit because he was so abusive to them. He did vile things to his children." They made it sound like it was sexual assault, and I was just horrified by a man abusing his family in this way. Before I went into his room, I centered myself and asked for spiritual guidance, like I did with every patient. I asked Creator and my spirit guides to help me say and do the right thing. I realized that I wasn't here to judge and suddenly I heard in my head, "go in and let him know he is loved and it is time to go home". I entered the room, and I held his hand and said he was safe, and that he was loved, and it was okay to let go and go home. Then this happened next. I felt and saw a light above my head come down through my head and out of my heart to this dying patient. I felt so much love encompass me and out to him that it brought tears to my eyes. I can't explain what happened, but I felt God was there with him. He died soon thereafter, and I know he is at peace.

OPENING YOUR HEART

*A**sk questions from your heart and you will be answered from the heart.* — Omaha Tribe

They are not dead who live in the hearts they leave behind — Tuscarora Proverb

An open heart is an essential component of walking the Red Road. Throughout this book, we will delve into additional teachings that will enhance and deepen your ability to open your heart, leading you to the profound and essential embodiment of love. When your heart is open, you can perceive the sacredness in all that surrounds you, and, in turn, you honor and respect your own sacred being. Open your heart to your brothers and sisters, the two and four-legged, Mother Earth, Creator, and listen. Whatever your religion or belief may be, open your heart. What do you hear, see, and feel? When you open your heart, you will awaken to the surrounding miracles. Popular culture often portrays spirituality as elusive, but in reality, it is more accessible than it seems. We are spiritual beings having a human experience, which inherently makes us spiritual. You may feel you are not a spiritual being based on "mistakes" from the past, but that is a false belief. Some people may find spirituality challenging, as they perceive it to be too intricate, deceptive, or contradictory. Religion's dogmas can deter people from spirituality. Reflect on your personal meaning of spirituality.

This book will serve as a valuable companion on your spiritual path, helping you to explore and deepen your connection to Spirit. We believe in keeping spirituality simple and uncomplicated. At its core, we feel spirituality involves embracing the profound impact of an open heart that allows us to recognize and experience a deep sense of interconnectedness. When we reach that feeling, we realize that every step we take is sacred. We begin to honor and respect the entire universe as a sacred gift. These teachings are to remind you that spirituality is all around and within you. It's not about dogma, it's about connection. If we don't feel connection, our heart closes, creating blockages. Think about how and when your heart became closed. What if you find it difficult to open your heart back up? Perhaps you have experienced abuse or had a major loss or difficulty in your life? Regardless of past or future difficulties, remember you're not alone. Many people have had similar experiences. The truth is, life can be difficult. We all experience losses, hurt, and sadness that closed our hearts, but one way or the other, most move forward from the pain. There are times we forget we are spirit. The question is, when we forget, how do we open up our hearts and remember this important lesson?

Opening your heart after it has been closed takes time. Have patience and take small, gradual steps. One way to open your heart is to take the time to listen and observe nature. As you observe nature, you may feel a sense of peace and connection to something greater than yourself. Let yourself be inspired by the resilience and beauty of the natural world, and allow that inspiration to guide you in opening your heart to others and to yourself. There are many teachers in nature if we just reach out to them. Even nurturing a pet or having that pet be your companion can open your heart. Take them for a walk or play with them. Our furry friends open our hearts in so many ways!

Understand that your heart is the gateway to the highest vibrational frequency, providing a pathway for connection and alignment. When you connect to higher vibrations, it brings healing into your form. Tuning into higher frequencies fosters healing, while aligning with lower frequencies lead to stress. Vibrations are part of everything in existence and it's also how we perceive the world around us. Everything in the universe, including our thoughts, emotions, and physical surroundings, emits vibrations that can affect our energy and well-being. Our senses, such as touch, hearing, and sight, rely on detecting vibrations in the environment. Our ears detect vibrations traveling through the air, creating the sense of sound. Our sense of vision relies on vibrations of light entering our eyes. Even taste and smell are based on the vibrations of molecules interacting with receptors in our mouth and nose. Life is connected through vibrations. From the smallest cells in our body to the vast expanse of the universe, everything is constantly vibrating. Understanding and connecting to vibrations enhances our connection to ourselves and the world. The trees, rocks, animals, thoughts, words, emotions...everything! As you elevate your vibration, your heart opens, leading to increased happiness and decreased anxiety. Everything you are reading in this book will help you open your heart to reach the highest vibration — that of love.

Sometimes we forget that our thoughts, beliefs, and how we view the world influence our vibration. Kevin Todeschi, author of *Spirit in Motion*, and an expert on Edgar Cayce's readings, suggests that vibrations are essentially spirit in motion, and our thoughts and actions profoundly influence our lives and how we experience them. He explains that ... "People also affect one another (both consciously and unconsciously, and positively and negatively) with their personal vibration. On the negative end of the spectrum, someone that is angry, depressed, negative, or somehow 'draining' to be around. On the positive end of the spectrum is someone who is most often optimistic, inspirational, or genuinely spiritual can come across as an individual who, be her or his very presence, is motivational, nurturing, compassionate, or even a healing presence. In fact, the possibility of possessing such a heightened vibration that it can somehow positively impact and raise the vibrations in another person, facilitating healing in the process, is described in scripture on numerous occasions." 4 That's powerful knowing that the people we know can bring healing or disease.

Take a moment to reflect on your life. Do you want to be with friends or family that are always complaining about life, or would you rather hang with someone looking at the best outcomes in situations? Think of someone you know that is usually positive about their life. Now think of someone you know that is often negative. Do you believe that life delivers sour apples to one and not the other? Most times, their lives are probably similar; it is their perception of their life that differs. They are choosing to put either optimism or pessimism into their form. If you are the one always complaining, having this awareness helps open your heart to better choices. All life has positives and negatives. The question is...where do you want to put your attention? Focus on the highest vibrations and your heart will open. Shift your perception and start witnessing miracles.

Wakan Tanka, Great Mystery, teach me how to trust my heart, my mind, my intuition, my knowing, the sense of my body, the blessings of my spirit. Teach me to trust these things so that I may enter my Sacred Space and love beyond my fear, and thus Walk in Balance with the passing of each glorious sun.

— Lakota Prayer

Indigenous people live an open-hearted lifestyle filled with gratitude for the Great Spirit and all elements of their surroundings. Gratitude changes your perception of the world, revealing its true beauty. You start hearing the voices of the trees and animals around you — you feel their essence. You understand what they are communicating and realize they are there to help in your journey. It is time to awaken and embrace nature and life with open hearts. To listen with wholehearted attention. Once we start to fill our heart with all the greatness that the world literally has to offer, great things will come into our life. Teachers will appear to you in many forms, including the animals and plant life. The world is already in perfect order; it has many teachings and lessons if we just listen and stop messing it up. There are so many healings that are provided for us, such as plant medicine to help cure diseases or help with symptoms. Native Americans used herbal remedies, sourced from their natural surroundings, as a crucial part of their healing practice. They saw herbs and medicinal plants as deeply sacred. You had to open your heart to the medicine. You had to see the plant. Alongside plant healings, Native American communities commonly united in ceremonies, dances, prayer, drumming, and chanting to aid an ill individual. It was a natural existence, living in harmony with the plants and animals.

Reflect on what makes your heart sing. What are you passionate about? The ideas and possibilities are limitless. Work with animals, plant a garden, volunteer, join a group, play or listen to music, sew, practice yoga, sail, fish, keep a journal or explore different local activities. Create your own group, like a book club or game night. When you open up to what you are passionate about, you are naturally raising your vibration, thereby opening your heart. Stop making excuses about time or money. Count how many hours you spend scrolling your apps or watching TV. Time is available to everyone and numerous activities are affordable or free. Maybe you dream of visiting Italy but don't have the money. Save a few dollars every week. So what if it takes ten years?

In the meantime, buy a book that examines Italian culture or study the language. Join an Italian club or cooking class. We are a society of wanting immediate gratification and give up on our dreams if we can't grasp them right away. Don't give up on your dreams. Ever. Passion and joy will help you bring forth an open heart. Be patient with life and yourself. Lead an authentic, positive, loving life. Our daily thoughts define our identity. Use the analogy of comparing a loving heart to a pilot light on a gas stove. The flame stays lit, as does your heart's love, but it's your responsibility to increase the flame. We believe we all have a responsibility to ourselves and others to be encouraging, loving, respectful, and honorable. Don't allow anyone to blow out your pilot light or dishonor you. What resonates with you may not resonate with your family or friends. Look at your life as your own book you write. Others can have input, but you are the author. More importantly, just go out and live!

In summary, opening your heart allows you to see the spiritual medicines that are within and around you. When you have an open heart, it's easier to navigate the Good Red Road. Sometimes our heart closes, and during those times, we experience pain. Look for ways to open your heart. This can manifest in different ways, like discovering your passion or observing and learning from nature. It's time to take action. Embrace the love that you are meant to be!

Larry's Aha Moment

My heart is open to the forgotten people, the Native Americans that walked on this earth long ago. I've taken on the responsibility of taking care of their sacred grounds. I have and continue to have many ceremonies at these sacred sites, and I am in constant prayer for my ancestors. One night when I was out praying, visions along with the silence of the wind came to me, and I made a promise to all the spirit people that night that I would take on this responsibility because my heart was so open. For too many years, the remains of Native Americans have been dishonored and disgraced by removing their remains from their sacred resting place. I am in the process of raising funds for the construction of a monument on the second largest sacred Native American burial grounds in Corpus Christi, Texas, to honor our ancestors, whose remains have been disturbed and exhumed. It is my hope and dream that my continued work will draw the support of people from all nations and walks of life to open up hearts and help with this cause.

One of my first experiences of truly opening up my heart to the fullest is when my children came forth into the world. When they were born, I realized they were part of my essence, part of my ancestors. I remember the day I made a solemn promise to Creator to do everything in the world to teach and protect them, and I'm continuing to do so in their adult lives. I constantly ask myself what teachings I can leave on this earth so that they can be proud of their father. My children continue to open up my heart in ways that are unimaginable to me.

I was raised by a loving and wonderful stepfather who came into my life when I was six years old and taught me many spiritual lessons. He, in every sense of the word, was my father. I never had a relationship with my biological father, so I continue to be empathetic to those children who do not have a father taking part in their lives. I have spiritually adopted and continue to mentor many children. I have committed myself to their well- being and they, in turn, open up my heart as well. I volunteer my teachings to the community, which includes schools, so children are a big part of my life. I believe children see through the eyes of God, and we can learn many lessons from them.

There are many teachable moments with children. One example is when I first started hosting a drum circle in Corpus Christi, Texas. I noticed that there were quite a few women interested in coming to the drum with their children. What I soon learned was that some men were not taking responsibility to help their children learn the Native ways. The women were the one stepping up to the teachings of the drum. Drumming for women and their children opened up so many hearts and connected them to Native songs and lessons.

I continue to reach out to many people from all walks of life, including the hopeless, the untouchables, and the unwanted. I've taken on responsibilities for many gravesites where their loved ones are not able to visit or are no longer around to visit. I continually pray for all people daily and answer all personal requests for prayer.

Pam's Aha Moment

I would like to share a magical encounter with a hummingbird that opened my heart to all creatures, large and small. When my son was young, we had a small patio and pool area where many of our friends and their children gathered. I noticed a hummingbird making its nest in a wind chime directly in front of me, where I sat on the patio. I remember thinking how strange it was for the hummingbird to build a nest right in the middle of all this activity. But it was a blessing for me because every day I would sit in my chair and talk lovingly to the hummingbird as she built her nest. Soon she was sitting on her egg and then feeding her baby. I enjoyed sitting outside talking and watching her.

One morning when I was inside the house, the frantic movement of the mother hummingbird distracted me outside my patio door. She was dive-bombing the patio table and ringing the wind-chimes and flying right at the sliding door. I knew she was trying to get my attention, and that something was wrong. I ran outside, and she quickly flew toward the pool and skimmed an area on top of the water. As I looked down, there was her baby floating in the pool. (My eyes are tearing as I write this story). I scooped out the baby, and as I tried to pump her tummy gently, she looked dead. My husband came out and stated the baby was dead. I was devastated and felt so helpless. I remember saying out loud that the mother would know what to do, so I put its lifeless body into the nest. The mother worked on the baby. She put her beak down the baby's throat and continued to work frantically. After what felt like an eternity, the mother brought the baby back to life. I was filled with so much joy! The following moment is forever etched in my memory. The mother flew down to me and just hovered in front of me and then flew up to her baby. She continued to hover at eye level and then fly to her baby. She was thanking me! That summer, she and her baby followed me around and would land next to me while I spoke lovingly to both mother and child. I was truly honored that she put her faith in me and trusted that I would "listen." I heard Mother Earth smile that day.

Animals seem to come into my life. I've had hummingbirds fly into the house, and I gently retrieve them and carry them outside. I've experienced a young red-tail hawk sit on my lap and just stare at me. My husband looks at me dumbfounded and I just smile. Open your heart and talk to them. They can hear you! In 2005, I left Flagstaff, Arizona, and moved to Texas. I had received many teachings in Flagstaff, and I wanted to give thanks to my many spirit and animal guides for their teachings over the years. My husband and a good friend accompanied me. As

I was conducting the ceremony, birds of various species flew down and sat in the trees near the water. Some perched and just listened. I burned sage and gave thanks to the four sacred directions, Mother Earth and Creator. As I ended the ceremony, the birds flew off. The timing and presence of the birds amazed us. It was as if they were coming to say goodbye and thank you. I felt that Mother Earth and her children received my gratitude.

SYNCHRONICITY

*S*ynchronicity is choreographed by a great, pervasive intelligence that lies at the heart of nature, and is manifested in each of us through intuitive knowledge.
— Deepak Chopra

Listen to the air. You can hear it, feel it, smell it, taste it. Woniya Wakan—the holy air—renews all by its breath. Woniya Woniya Wakan—spirit, life, breath renewal—it means all that. Woniya—we sit together, don't touch, but something is there; we feel it between us, as a presence. A good way to start thinking about nature, talk about it. Rather talk to it, talk to the rivers, to the lakes, to the winds as to our relatives.
— John (Fire) Lame Deer

Awaken and journey into the synchronistic energy of the universe and witness more and more miracles. Synchronistic events help guide us to open our vessel to our soul's purpose. These events help point us in the right direction if only we stop and take notice. Recognizing synchronicity is an important component of our spiritual medicines. Maybe you keep seeing the same repeated numbers, animals, images, words, or other events? That is the Universe, Creator, and spirit guides communicating with you. They are accompanying you on your journey, offering encouragement to continue on the path you are on and expressing their desire to share in memorable experiences with you. Even during tough moments, they're there offering support and encouragement to help you navigate the Good Red Road. Everything in life is alive and trying to communicate. Our task is to remain attuned to the synchronicities that surround us, always ready to listen and interpret the messages they convey.

The signs and messages that hold significance are often right in front of us, ready to guide us, yet sometimes we may overlook them. Have you heard the lesson-filled story about the man caught in a flood? As the water levels started rising on his street, neighbors came by in a boat and urged him to evacuate, warning him of the imminent flooding that would soon engulf the entire town. He declined because he was going to trust the Lord to save him. As the floodwaters continued to rise, forcing him to seek safety on the second floor, another boat arrived, offering to rescue him. Despite their pleas, he adamantly refused, proclaiming God would save him. The water continued to rise, and he climbed onto his roof. A helicopter flew over and the crew said, "Take this line—we will save you!" Again he said no, that God was going to save him. As the waters rose even higher, they swept him away, and he drowned. He went before God and he asked, "God, why didn't you save me?" God answered, "Who do you think sent the two boats and a helicopter?" The lesson to be learned is that God may work through ordinary people and resources to provide aid in times of need. Holding on to expectations can prevent you from noticing the synchronicities.

Various spiritual and religious traditions offer unique perspectives on the concept of synchronicity. Some belief systems view synchronicity as a manifestation of divine guidance, while others may see it as evidence of interconnectedness. Some individuals may view synchronicity as seemingly random events that hold personal significance. Interpretations vary, reflecting diverse beliefs about reality, but whatever your belief, no one can deny these events take place in our lives.

Carl Jung, Swiss psychiatrist and psychotherapist, was the first person to define the concept of synchronicity. Synchronicity, as defined by Carl Jung, refers to the occurrence of meaningful coincidence of two or more events where something other than the probability of chance is involved. Jung believed synchronicities are manifestations of the underlying interconnectedness of the universe and the collective unconscious. He saw synchronicity as a way to access deeper layers of the psyche and gain insight into one's own inner workings and the mysteries of existence.5

Perhaps it was divine guidance that led you to cross paths with a specific person or to end up sitting next to them on a bus. Maybe a book that you happened to stumble upon was actually divinely orchestrated to enter your life at just the right moment and bring about a profound transformation within you. Reflect on your life and consider the individuals who have impacted you, or whom you have helped in times of need. It could have been a word, deed, or gesture that sparked a synchronistic event. There are many personal examples of synchronicities that might have had a lasting impact on your beliefs, perspectives, and actions, leading you on a journey of self-discovery that changed the course of your life.

An impactful article on synchronicity recounted a story from a "Dear Ann" letter. A man wrote Dear Ann as an adult, but his story took place when he was in high school. The man poured his heart out in the letter, describing the depths of his despair during his adolescence, when he felt consumed by sadness and weighed down by thoughts of ending his own life. In fact, one morning he said he had made a plan to end his life after school. He told Ann on his chosen day he accidentally dropped his books in the school hallway and a boy his age helped picked them up. They talked while picking up the books, and the boy asked if he wanted to walk home with him. They walked home, so he postponed his suicide that day. The next day the boy came over to visit, and again, he postponed his suicide. The postponements continued, and the two boys became friends, and soon the man said he was no longer suicidal. That one act of kindness, helping someone pick up some dropped books, led to a friendship and saved a boy's life. The man said he lost contact with his friend as an adult, and he had never told his friend how he literally saved his life. Was that a synchronistic moment? The man believes it was. We do too. Realize the impact you have on people. You are intervening in a spiritual way that you might not be conscious of. Remember, we are always connected with spirit. You might say the right word, be in the right place, do the right thing at the exact moment because of the spiritual connection to help that particular person. We are all spirit, so we are working as angels in disguise. Did meeting your best friend or partner lead you on a soulful journey? Maybe you found that special pet that was meant to come into your life to provide comfort and friendship. Contemplate on your life and its synchronistic moments.

Synchronicity can come in many forms, including warnings, red flags, or an internal communication that tells us not to do a certain thing or proceed on a particular path. There might be times when we ignore the warnings, and against our better judgment, we've crossed our fingers and wished for the best when our intuition told us otherwise. We may have continued forward only to realize that we should have trusted our intuition. Can you think of a time where you said, "I knew that was going to happen"? There are times we discount our intuition, not placing much emphasis on its accuracy. We might question, how can we trust our intuition if we can't even measure it? Some people view intuition as an overactive imagination. However, Albert Einstein once said, "Imagination is everything. It is the preview of life's coming attractions."

What about people who scoff at synchronicity, calling it frivolous; saying it has no merit without scientific proof or backing? Have you witnessed people so tightly wound they look like they're about to explode? People who are so structured that anything out-of-order causes so much anxiety? They try to control every detail, eventually disrupting life's natural flow. How can we understand the interconnectedness of all things when we try to control everything around us? It's counter intuitive and can leave us feeling anxious. When we are tightly wrapped, we don't recognize or allow the miracles of life to unfold in front of us. We become so intense that we can't enjoy the joy of being. Our society has taken on too many nonsensical demands of perfection, not understanding the true meaning of life. Not only do we pressure ourselves, but we pressure our children as well. We've somehow allowed this unbalanced teaching to take form, putting pressure on every detail of daily living.

Our society exhibits an unbalanced fixation on the concept of time. The clock often dictates our routines, making it necessary for us to adhere to the constraints of time and society. Effectively managing our time is critical in various aspects of our lives, helping us prioritize tasks, achieve goals, and maintain a healthy work-life balance. However, in a fast-paced society where busyness is often glorified, we may find ourselves overwhelmed with commitments and responsibilities, leaving us feeling restless during moments of downtime. It's important to find balance. How can we awaken to life's wonders if we never slow down? How can we open up to the synchronistic events of the universe if we plan and account for every second of the day? Where is there room for anything else to take place?

How can one enhance the perception of synchronistic occurrences in this fast-paced world? What techniques are available to us? One technique is to practice mindfulness. Mindfulness helps you open and recognize the signs and signals that are always around you. It leads to a deeper understanding of the environment and of yourself. This heightened awareness can help you navigate life with more clarity and insight and respond to situations more intentionally. Mindfulness is such a significant practice that we've devoted an entire chapter to exploring the concept.

How can we even see synchronicity if our mind is in constant thought, or our body is in constant motion? We wouldn't be able to recognize synchronicity if it hit us in the face. Edgar Cayce said, "Through prayer we speak to God. In meditation, God speaks to us."6 You don't have to take part in traditional meditation, just practice activities that help you quiet your mind. Some activities include reading, walking in nature, gardening, yoga, creative visualization, or other techniques to help deepen your connection to intuition.

Indigenous cultures were attuned and followed the rhythms of the seasons rather than adhering to structured time schedules. Living in harmony with nature necessitated adapting to the ever changing world around them. The Lakota Oyate closely observed the changes with each new moon and star pattern. They believed in meaningful coincidences and interconnectedness between natural phenomena and human experiences. By closely tracking the celestial events and their impact on the natural world, they sought to understand the deeper interconnectedness and harmony of the universe. This awareness of synchronicity helped them align their actions and decisions with the rhythms of nature and the cosmos.

Ceremonies commemorating seasonal changes are honored globally, demonstrating a continued recognition of their significance. In Japanese culture, the changing of the seasons is celebrated with festivals such as Hanami (cherry blossom viewing) in spring, and Tsukimi (moon viewing) in autumn. In Celtic culture, the Wheel of the Year marks the changing of seasons with eight festivals. These traditions help to connect people to the cycles of nature. In Native American culture, prayers and rituals often involve acknowledging and honoring the Four Directions (west, north, east, south). A Four Direction Ceremony involves making offerings and prayers to the spirits of the East, South, West, and North, each of which has its own unique symbolism and energy. Specific colors accompany the special meaning of the Four Directions, and the shape of the cross symbolizes all directions. The cross then signifies sustaining life, which serves as a reminder of keeping the balance of nature and its four elements. Native people were open to all the synchronistic events that unfolded around them, especially in nature. They understood the interconnection of all things in the universe and the value of respecting all life as sacred.

Open yourself up to the higher vibrations and synchronicities that are around you. Spirit is here to affirm your Red Road path or provide you with alternatives. Maybe there was a frustrating instance when you didn't get what you wanted. Then, some time later, you say, thank God that didn't happen...this result is much better. Trust the universe's flow and embrace your synchronistic messages. Be in the "is-ness." When we allow the universal flow to communicate with us, instead of letting our mind, body, and spirit go to places that are unhealthy, is when we are trusting and in perfect peace.

We can pick up positive and negative energies. Can you recall a time or place where you've felt instantly uncomfortable? Sometimes every fiber of our being tells us that something is not right. We need to listen to our quiet voice that speaks to us. There may be times we ignore or disregard our intuition when it is trying to bring forth messages to guide us. We might not even be sure which voice to listen to because our conscious mind is always in control and working overtime. One way to differentiate between the conscious mind and intuition is by paying attention to how the information is being processed. The conscious mind relies on logic, evidence, and reasoning to arrive at a conclusion, while intuition is more about trusting your instincts and gut feelings. The conscious mind can sometimes get caught up in negative thinking. It can manifest as self-doubt, worry, criticism, fear, and rumination of past mistakes or future uncertainties. This can lead to overthinking, doubt, and hesitation, causing us to ignore our instincts. Quieting the conscious mind is essential for peace to flow. By doing so, you can tap into your intuition. Cultivating and trusting our intuition is seen as a way to access our innate wisdom, connect with our higher self, and align with our divine nature. It is this source of wisdom, guidance and intuition that can help us navigate on the Red Road.

Practice quieting the voice that puts demands on you. We are in a habit of constant motion and frenzy. Stop, pause, or take a time out. It's commonly believed that quieting the mind requires years of practice, but just 5-10 minutes daily will establish a healthy habit. Since mindful activities are challenging to quantify, we often find ourselves drawn towards performance driven activities that emphasize action and productivity. We don't realize the importance of introspection and a quiet mind. Introspection helps us gain self-awareness, insight, and understanding of ourselves. It helps manages stress and navigates our life's challenges with greater clarity. Our culture has a tendency to look for answers from various media platforms. While social media platforms like Facebook can provide a way to connect with others and share experiences, they don't promote deep introspection or self-reflection. Our society has learned to thrive on validation from other people. Social media can bring about stress and frenzy, so it's important to balance with reflection and self-awareness. This self-awareness can help guide you in making choices and decisions that align with your authentic self. Think of a time when you felt peace. Where were you? What were you doing? How can you incorporate more of those moments into your life? When you feel calm and peaceful — hostility and anger dissipate. You will feel harmonious with the universe and synchronistic events will unfold, and people and animals will show up in your life. You will find inner peace despite the outer chaos. It is being aligned with the universe, allowing everything to fall into place.

We have all experienced unpleasant events in our life. Maybe these experiences led you to take on some bad habits? Well, how synchronistic is this book? It is important to acknowledge that at some point, everyone will encounter death, illness, or adversity, which will inevitably lead to a transformation in some aspect of our being. It forces a new perspective on life. We would never choose to learn from hardship if we had the choice. However, because of these hardships, there have been countless numbers of healing organizations started. This highlights the profound synchronicities that emerge from undergoing suffering or adversity. It's the love we have for our brothers and sisters. Through our pain, a phoenix is born, and our hearts connect with those who are suffering. Think about what has happened in your past and how that has made you the person you are today. Look at the people that have come from the streets, deeply addicted to drugs or alcohol, that now lead counseling classes that help others. The Great Spirit has ways to help us with our grief and problems if we are open to the synchronistic moments that are presented to us. There is always a solution for every problem. Never give up — you are never alone.

As we discussed earlier, animals can teach us important lessons. They play such a valuable role in promoting emotional and mental health, providing much needed companionship and comfort. Their unconditional love has a profound impact on our well-being and contributes to a sense of support and connection in challenging times. Maybe it's a symbiotic relationship where you both need healing? Nevertheless, they become our lifelong friends and companions. We could write a book just on the synchronistic events of animals alone. We honor the presence of dogs who fulfill unique and sacred roles, such as support dogs, therapy dogs, police dogs, service dogs, among other meaningful roles they fulfill. There are even dogs that sit on their owners' graves, refusing to leave. There are numerous heartwarming and inspiring stories of animals coming to the rescue and saving their owners' lives. One story in particular is about a pig that saved the owner's life when she was lying on the floor with a stroke. The pig went out through the doggy door and laid in the middle of the road. Most people drove around the pig, but one individual stopped. The pig led the man to the house where the woman was on the floor. The pig saved her life! There are countless other stories where animals have displayed similar bravery.

Animals are a significant part of synchronicity and they help us gather our spiritual medicines. You can go years without seeing a particular animal, but suddenly, they may come around because of your need for a particular healing, connection, or medicine. They know where to be and when to show up. Open your heart and accept Creator's gifts when they appear to you. Look at the healing that a particular animal brings to your life. Nature holds the power to heal. You might be drawn to water because it is often seen as a symbol of purity and spiritual power. Perhaps you are drawn to the forest because it is a source of wisdom and knowledge. What animals keep showing up in your life? What messages or lessons are they trying to teach you? Different animals carry different meanings and energies, and their presence can signal important messages or lessons you need to pay attention to. Awaken to what is in your path. It is no coincidence. Different animal guides come in and out of our lives, depending on what we need to complete our journey. We can also call on a specific animal depending on what medicine we need. What animal resonates with you? What do you believe their symbolic message conveys?

In summary, we all have synchronistic moments in our lives. When we quiet our minds, we can make room to awaken to these moments. Acknowledging these moments allows us to feel a deeper sense of connection, realizing that we are not alone on our journey. Spirit is all around us trying to communicate. Our Native brothers and sisters deeply understood that we are all interconnected and opened themselves up to the synchronicities of life. It is time to integrate these teachings into our being.

Larry's Aha Moment

Although I am close to all animals, for many years I went without a sacred animal to guide and help me. For starters, I wanted a bear or an eagle because my ego wanted great strength. Animals want to connect to us, but we, as people, have to do the greater part of opening up our heart. My power animal came to me in 1984 in a vision I had when I went to a sweat lodge. I never entertained the thought of going into the sweat lodge to get my sacred animal. My intent that day was to pray for a person who was dying.

While in the sweat lodge, I felt the heat of the steam from the rocks on my face. It was dark in the sweat lodge, so I couldn't see anything around me. Suddenly, I felt there was an animal standing right behind me. I actually felt its breath on my neck, and when I slightly turned around to see what it was, I saw a buffalo standing next to me. I was amazed to see this magnificent animal as we looked eye to eye at each other. The buffalo spoke in a language we could both understand, and it said, "I am to be your spirit guide. From this day forth, you will always keep my spirit around you and products around you to remind you of who I am and the strength I have provided to the people." The buffalo, many years ago, was the source of our people's lives. It provided everything for us, and we revere the buffalo. We gave it thanks and nurtured and honored it. When we took a buffalo's life, we honored its spirit so the spirit of the animal would live on. So I connected with the animal, and that day forward, I clearly understood who my sacred animal was. So now I surround myself with its products and my medicine bag has buffalo hair and drums with buffalo hide, and it gives me strength.

A few years ago, a buffalo was born, and the mother was rejecting it. They thought it was going to die, so they called me to look at the baby calf to honor it. We stayed there all night long, nurturing that calf back to health. To everyone's amazement, it survived, and it became attached to me, and I to it.

The buffalo gives me strength when I'm sad or doubtful, so I hang on to my bag and hold it close to me and draw its strength and power to help me through. Spirit animals can change. Sometimes we can keep the same spirit animal and then sometimes another animal needs to come to help you. Each animal represents its own power and teachings, and it is just according to where you are in your life depends on what particular animal comes forth. When we see a hummingbird all around us, it reminds us to be a service of the people, to be happy, free-flowing, and to bring forth joy.

Pam's Aha Moment

When I first decided to become a hospice nurse, it was a synchronistic moment. I had a dream where Clap Dance put me through a death ceremony. That dream led me to become a hospice nurse. I truly believe I was meant to be a hospice nurse and to help people cross over. When I was with a patient, I would always ask the Holy Spirit to help me, so I would say the right things to help patients and their loved ones in this difficult time. I was on-call one particular weekend where I visited another nurse's patient in the hospital. The first day of the visit, I walked into her room and she was comatose in bed, surrounded by family. I was planning to visit her the next day as well. That night, she came to me in my dream. We were both floating near the hospital ceiling looking down at her two daughters talking to the nurse at the nurses' station. The daughters were stressed and conflicted about discontinuing the tube feeding and thought they were being cruel, but knew it was their mother's wish. My hospice patient looked at me and told me to tell her daughters that it was an act of love, it honored her wishes, and she loved them very much. She appeared to me as a younger woman, and I clearly remembered how she looked even though she had no hair when I saw her. She had dark hair, parted in the middle, the ends curled upwards just below her chin. When I met with the family the next day, it was difficult for me to relay her message. I was a professional nurse and counselor. I didn't want to appear crazy or, worse, lose my job. However, I was instructed to relay the dream, so I complied. It turned out they were having conflicting feelings about discontinuing their mom's tube feeding and were extremely happy to receive her message. The daughter then pulled out a picture of their mom from her purse. There she was, looking exactly like I described to them in my dream—black hair, parted down the middle, and the ends curled up. It was validation from their mom.

Another Aha moment came when I lived in Europe. I tried to visit as many sacred sites as I could. I felt compelled to do so, as if maybe some of the sacredness would rub off on me or perhaps I would be told a message I could share. One special moment for me was in Greece when I visited the grotto where St. John wrote the Revelations. I "happened" to be alone for a few minutes. I was excited as I sat in the grotto in awe, and I thought how lucky I was to be in this sacred spot and have a moment to myself with God. As I sat there, I heard a voice inside me say, "You do not have to search for me. I am always with you." I realized at that moment I didn't have to search for God or his message — the Great Spirit is with all of us at all times.

My life has been full of synchronistic events, and my dreams, visions, and intuition have facilitated much of my actions and directions in life. However, synchronistic events don't just happen with dreams or voices; they are everywhere! We encourage you to open your heart to these messages. They can be in the form of a feather, coin, flower, butterfly, person, animal, thought, song, phone call, recurring number — there are countless examples!

Larry and Pam's Synchronistic Moment Together

Larry and I have been like brother and sister for many years, and we had a blood brother and sister ceremony to make it official. During and after the ceremony, many synchronistic events happened. The first synchronistic happening was the scheduling of the ceremony. Larry was visiting our fishing lodge, and we just picked a morning one week to conduct the ceremony. When we watched the weather on TV the night before, it turned out that evening was a full moon and a lunar eclipse was to start at sunrise when we were to perform the ceremony.

The second synchronistic event happened after the pipe ceremony. As you put the pipe away, you disconnect the pipe and bowl with a blessing. Just as Larry separated the pipe, a great wind blew in. Serenity enveloped the entire ceremony, bringing a sense of tranquility. When Larry's mother passed away, he adopted the wind as his mother, and we felt she was blessing us.

Next, during the conclusion of the ceremony, an eagle rode the breeze in and circled Larry and me about twenty-five or thirty feet above us. It made one circle and then left. Larry and I put our left hand on our heart and then out to the eagle. It was such a blessing that we will never forget.

The events of that special day kept happening. While we drove to town to print out some pictures of our ceremony, we saw a baby fawn at the side of the road. What a beautiful sight, and we just looked at her and then at each other in awe. On the way back from the store, we saw a chupacabra type animal on the same road running into the woods. We couldn't believe our eyes, but we both witnessed its appearance. All these synchronistic events unfolding right in front of us amazed us.

That night, talking about the sacred event and our new brother/sister relationship, we sat gazing at the orange grandmother moon. And the icing on the cake was when my husband found the piece of leather with my name, Two Spirits. The date on it was exactly two years prior to our brother and sister's ceremony. Now how synchronistic is that?

RETURNING OF THE ANCESTORS
RECLAIMING FEMININE POWER

The "Returning of the Ancestors" was a ceremony that took place in Northern Arizona in April 2009. A Mayan priest initiated the ceremony. He gathered Holy Men to share prophecies, teachings, prayers, and ceremonies cherished for centuries. Organizers invited 150 Holy Men and Wisdom Keepers from across the globe. Larry Running Turtle was honored when the organizers asked him to be one of the 150 to attend this sacred ceremony. The gathering was open to all brothers and sisters of all different faiths, beliefs, and cultures. Thousands of people came to receive these prophecies and spiritual messages.

Six Holy Men, from diverse lands, recorded their prophecies on paper. They brought their prophecies to share with the Medicine Men and Wisdom Keepers from around the world, and all who would listen. One evening, a circle formed around the six Holy Men as they dropped their prophecies into the sacred circle. One man stepped forward into the sacred circle and began reading the prophecies aloud. Some were convinced that the world's end or other ominous happenings were imminent. However, this was not the case. Not one prophecy indicated the end of the world. To the amazement of all, all six prophecies, originating from different corners of the world, shared a remarkably unified message. The six messages conveyed to all that great change was on the way. It was inevitable. This change would not emerge out of chaos and drama, but in the way of reconnecting with Mother Earth. Most importantly, it would be the female who would make this happen. The female energy was going to excel and explode with a great deal of power because the men have messed up the world long enough. The attendees were advised to bring forth feminine energies in order to heal Mother Earth.

In order to save the planet, we must tap into the powerful and nurturing energy of the feminine. A lot of women intuitively understand and feel Mother Earth and her pain. They have an innate connection to Mother Earth because they are the givers of life and nurturers of the land. They have the capacity to create and sustain life, which is reflected in the cycles of nature and the interconnectedness of all living beings. Women often have a deep appreciation for the beauty and abundance of Mother Earth and feel a sense of responsibility to care for and protect the environment. This spiritual connection can be seen in the rituals, ceremonies, and traditions that many cultures have that honor and celebrate the natural world. Women tap into a source of strength, wisdom, and guidance from the pulse of our Mother which allows us to navigate the balances of life. Women are able to pick up on subtle cues and emotions, making them great communicators and caregivers. Their ability to empathize allows for connection with others on a deeper level of understanding. They excel at being collaborative visionaries and are protectors of the earth. It's not all sweet, though; women can be like mama bears that fiercely protect their cubs. They have a significant influence on the young ones and provide the lessons needed to live in a complex world. We urgently need feminine compassion and selflessness, and it is important to acknowledge that men have the capacity to embody these qualities as well. There are many men capable of nurturing and serving as the primary loving role models for their children. This is not about gender; it is about energies. Both genders possess a blend of feminine and masculine energies within them. It is important to balance and integrate both energies to create a sense of wholeness and harmony. However, it is prophesied that in order to restore harmony and protect Mother Earth, it is essential to honor and amplify the nurturing, intuitive, and creative energies often associated with the feminine aspect of the divine. Men have the opportunity to access and embody feminine energies if they choose to open their hearts.

The Clan Mothers ran everything and had the last word. I think that's the answer.
— Floyd Red Crow Westerman

Native American culture has a rich history of women taking part in ceremonial life. Women took on many roles, and in certain tribes, they took part in drum and pipe ceremonies. The drum is female, its heartbeat is from Mother Earth. The drum in many cultures is a female symbol representing creativity, nurturing and the rhythm of life. The sacred pipe, bestowed by White Buffalo Calf Woman, holds divine healing power. If it wasn't for White Buffalo Calf Woman, the Native Americans wouldn't have the pipe today and how it connects with Christ himself. Maybe people will finally awaken to what the Native Americans knew all along. We need to listen, respect, and honor women. Native women played critical roles in passing down ancestral knowledge and they were very adept at medicinal herbs and farming as well. Because of their strength and wisdom, some even negotiating peace treaties. Women were essential to the overall functioning of the tribe. Some native women also held roles as chiefs and spiritual leaders. For example, some experienced Cherokee women could sit on councils. The "Council of Grandmothers" even had authority to nullify the Chief's decisions. Today, tribes still honor their women in powwows, sweat lodges, and in many other ways.

We wish to bring attention to the long-standing issue of missing and murdered indigenous women. The Urban Indian Health Institute statistics state that murder is the third leading cause of death for Native women. What makes this difficult is the lack of adequate help because of ongoing poverty and lack of tribal jurisdiction. What amplifies the situation is that negative stereotypes of Native people persist, causing a lack of media coverage typically given to white victims. Lately, grassroots efforts, mostly spearheaded by women, have brought about increased political attention, but it is important to stress that this situation remains horrific. Please stay informed by googling Native Hope, an organization that helps raises awareness and works toward justice through providing platforms, tools and resources. hope@native-hope.org (888) 999-2108

Women all over the world we ask you to stand, recognize, and reclaim your power. It's horrifying to see women still facing discrimination and repression in our modern world. Recent legislative measures increasingly appear to be restricting women's rights and opportunities. Society continues to perpetuate patriarchal and misogynistic beliefs, often portraying women as incapable, incompetent, or lesser than men. In many cultures, women's voices continue to be suppressed, and worse — killed because of their views. Young girls who merely attended school in Iran suffered mass poisonings in 2022. It's hard to imagine that this is still prevalent in some societies. It's undeniable that in advanced countries like the United States, we've made significant progress. However, we need to do more for women's rights and fair treatment. Compare the number of male CEOs to women or just pay scales for that matter. People often view women displaying empathy and compassion in business as a weakness. The perception that doing the right thing in business is feminine and weak is a harmful stereotype that perpetuates a culture of unethical behavior and greed. We need to challenge outdated gender stereotypes and reframe the narrative to recognize the strength and value of feminine traits in business. By promoting empathy, integrity, and ethical decision-making, we can create a more sustainable and inclusive business environment that benefits not only the bottom line, but society as a whole. Haven't we poisoned and damaged enough of our world? For the sake of our children's children, it's time to incorporate feminine energy to our planet in order to save her.

The world is in an unhealthy state and change is imminent due to our actions. Mother Earth is a living being and she will protect herself. Climate change, environmental degradation, social inequity, political unrest, and global health crises are interconnected and intertwined, posing a threat to both humanity and the planet. Indigenous people have been shouting the message that the far and wide transgression on Mother Earth will ultimately bring disaster. We have been listening with deaf ears and tragic events will continue. There are consequences to all our disrespect and destruction. We can't emphasize this enough. Women are vital to sustaining the planet. We hope you take your place of honor, and awaken to how powerful you are. So, women, please try to observe your ways. Those of you who are reading this right now we ask you this. Do you lower your worth? Are you displaying confidence as a woman or do you defer to men even though your intuition and heart tell you differently? Can you continue to take a backseat and let this patriarchal society ruin the world? It is time to throw your shoulders back and know your words and actions matter. Know that you are natural nurturers and teachers of all things, large and small. Feel the part of you that is connected to the pulse of Mother Earth. You are the medicine women, the ones that gather the medicine for your family. Can't you look into the eyes of your child, partner, or friend and tell when they are sick? You are intuitive and wise and know Mother Earth is hurting. Start to awaken and take responsibility for what you know deep inside of you. You are givers of sacred life and are grounded in Mother Earth and connected to Father Sky. The essence of life is found in the sacred and interconnected nature of family, where all lives hold meaning. Without you, there is no future.

Men's inherent ego and competitiveness have long driven this world. Look at the negative impact the male energy has manifested. We continue to have conflicts, poison the earth and sky; we even poison the foods we eat. Mother Earth continues to be raped of her resources as we passively watch these things unfold. Mother Earth is suffering, and we let it happen. We pray for feminine energies to bring forth compassion to nurture and heal her wounds. Women must take their rightful place in this world. We are asking women to take steps by teaching your husbands, brothers, fathers, and sons to be more compassionate.

No longer must the almighty dollar be our God. Think about what you are leaving behind for the children of the earth. Don't be afraid to use your words no matter what the circumstances. Stand tall and take your rightful place. Every slight gesture, word, or lesson adds up!

Men, embrace your feminine energies because the world needs you to step up to the plate. You must incorporate compassion, put down your weapons, and do the right thing. The time has come to align with moral values. It is written in the prophecy that female energy will bring about great change in the world. We have built a society that is mostly based on power, competition, ego, and money, but we now need everyone's help to save humanity. A new paradigm must take shape in our society for our future survival. We must practice sustainable resource management by replenishing what we extract from the earth. There are long-term repercussions of our actions. Again, put ego, power, the need to be right, and competition aside, and simply do the right things. We need to speak for the trees, the rocks, and all living things. Everything is alive and has spirit. We are all interconnected. Ask yourself this, "What am I leaving behind?" Women encourage and reinforce the men to embrace their female energies and let them understand they do not have to be forceful in their ways. Teach them to listen with their heart. When men are embracing their feminine energies, encourage them. There is nothing better than encouragement.

Women reclaim your power as a woman, without feeling the need to conform to the unrealistic expectations of being a "supermom." Nourish yourselves and honor your spirit without running yourselves ragged. To overextend is forgetting your original instruction to honor yourselves. Never feel guilty for speaking your truth or doing what's right. If enough women stand together, the message will be heard. Your background, experiences, and past narratives might have you stuck in false, negative, or insecure thinking of being powerless. Release the misconception that feminine energies are not intelligent or worthy. When you remove these illusions, you start to see higher aspects of yourself.

Yes, it is scary, but don't walk in fear. You might have been taught that you should be coy and cute, maybe even display helplessness so men on white horses can come and rescue you. Do you remember similar storylines on TV and in movie theaters? The poor female stuck in a castle by some unknown force, when a strong and smart man comes and rescues her. False narratives were also told about Native Americans. They were portrayed as savages and lost in their ways until the White Man rescued them and forced their teachings on them. Don't live by outdated rules and paradigms. The trend is healthier and more uplifting, but we still have a long way to go.

To summarize, it is prophesied that feminine energies will bring forth healing and save humanity. The sacred energy and healing wisdom of women are essential in the collective effort to harness spiritual medicines and safeguard the sacred balance of Mother Earth. We all must embody a new consciousness of a more loving and connected planet. We have destroyed too much in the name of power, ego, and money. Humanity must embrace feminine energies in order for the world to survive.

Larry's Aha Moment

I embraced my feminine energy at an early age. My mom, who taught me many lessons, brought me up. She taught me the importance of honoring women and the process of birth and creation. My mom ingrained in me the importance of honoring and respecting women. I was taught that all people are equal, all people. My mom also taught me the beauty of artwork, and to this day, that is my profession. I'm honored to have had my mom in my life, despite her passing. I still remember her teachings. Now when I want to visit my mom who has passed away, I now whisper in the wind.

When I drum, we always honor Mother Earth and women. Women are a big part of our drumming circle in Corpus Christi. We honor these women and sing songs for these women. As should be, my elders granted me permission to allow women to take part in the drum circle. Men were not stepping up to the plate and taking responsibility in teaching their children the Native ways. The women were coming around the drum circle bringing their children, and I welcomed them. They are a big part of our drum circle, and I honor them. In my medicine bag, I carry relics of ancient ones that were female to give me their strength. I call on them to help me in today's world. The world is shifting towards female energies and should keep doing so. Men have ruined the world, now it's time for female energies to take charge. Our only route to salvation is by preserving Mother Earth and standing united with our brothers and sisters. Now is the time.

Pam's Aha Moment

In our first book, I wrote about the time I used my voice with the help of paraphrasing Chief Seattle to stand up for Mother Earth when there was a proposal that would negatively impact the small amount of National Forest in East Texas. As we walk the Red Road together, we can all use our voice along the way to make ourselves, families, and communities a better place. We all matter! For my part in this Aha Moment, I would like to recognize, acknowledge, honor and thank all women reading this book right now. I know there were times you needed to stand up for yourself or others and use your voice. Even if it was simply teaching your children or others how to be kind, or a simple please and thank you. This is a strong medicine. I know there are many examples where you used your voice. Reflect on a time when you demonstrated courage, resilience, or compassion, and acknowledge the strength and growth those experiences brought you. Your voice and teachings matter.

There are so many brave and diverse women and so many in history as well. Just think about how our ancestors helped us forge ahead with the right to vote. There are Native Women, such as Zitkala-Sa (Red Bird/Gertrude Simmons Bonnin), who lectured across the country promoting the preservation of Native American cultural and tribal identities. While critical of assimilation, she staunchly believed Indigenous Americans should be American citizens and have the right to vote. She worked with White suffrage groups and was active in the General Federation of Women's Clubs beginning in 1921.

Mourning Dove was a Salish Indian, and she was the first Native American woman to write and publish novels. She states, "everything on this earth has a purpose, every disease an herb to cure it, and every person a mission. This is the Indian theory of existence."

Countless women, from all cultures, have made and continue to make a difference. I encourage you to google and explore the inspiring history of women's achievements. Explore your local libraries and museums. I guarantee you they are chock full of stories of the accomplishments made by women. We also want to recognize the silent women who tirelessly give back without acknowledgment. We thank and honor you. For the women that held families together, helped sick children (or furry children), we thank and honor you. We see you, the women who gathers medicine, with a discerning gaze that reflects both knowledge and empathy, capable of understanding and alleviating pain. Please acknowledge all the strong medicine you bring forth to your family and community. You are the true gatherers of spiritual medicines and we honor you.

TEACHINGS COME IN MANY FORMS

L *isten to all the teachers in the woods. Watch the trees, the animals, and all living things—you'll learn more from them than from books.*
— Joe Coyhis, Stockbridge-Munsee

One thing to remember is to talk to the animals. If you do, they will talk back to you. But if you don't talk to the animals, they won't talk back to you, then you won't understand, and when you don't understand you will fear, and when you fear you will destroy the animals, and if you destroy the animals, you will destroy yourself.
— Chief Dan George, Tsleil-Waututh

Teachings come in many forms throughout our lifetime, and we need to open our heart to these teachings and the teachers who deliver them. The teachings can include people, animals and even the challenging situations we encounter. We can learn valuable lessons from all life's experiences if we are open to listening and growing. Knowing that life is a spiritual journey helps us to open our hearts to the sacred teachings that are all around us. Sometimes we get caught up with everyday drama of life and identify with our human qualities and forget that we are spirits having a human experience. Getting caught up with drama is so easy that we overlook valuable spiritual teachings, fixating on trivial matters instead. What we often worry about in the present will probably be insignificant in the future. It's important to keep things in perspective and not let temporary anxieties overshadow the bigger picture. The change in perspective we experience from our lessons allows us to become more resilient, grounded, and flexible, like grandfather tree. Learning from life makes later years productive and exciting. We've learned to put into practice the serenity prayer: "God grant me the serenity to accept the things I cannot change, the courage to change the things I can, and the wisdom to know the difference." If we embrace the serenity concept, we ourselves become teachers and role models for our children and other people as well. We realize then, we are both teacher and student. Cultivating serenity within ourselves adds value and depth to our lives as we grow older. Older individuals can serve as invaluable mentors and sources of wisdom. Many cultures have high regard for their elders. Honoring the elders is one of the original instructions of Native Americans. In Native American culture, people respect and revere elders as exceptional teachers, valuing their wisdom and guidance. They are the Wisdom Keepers, and the biggest libraries of Indian knowledge, history, and tradition. They hold a special place in the community and are often consulted for advice and guidance on important matters. Elders are spiritual leaders and are called upon to perform important ceremonies and rituals.

In *To Build a Bridge: Working with American Indian Communities*, authors John Poupart and John Red Horse affirm that, "cultural values have been the source of strength for Indian people for many centuries."7 It is widely acknowledged that Native American elders have always been revered for their wisdom and continue to be held in high esteem today.

In Asian cultures, elders are also honored and celebrated. For example, in Korea, the 60th and 70th birthdays are prominent life events, celebrated with large parties and feasts. They are celebrated for their contributions to the family and society. Overall, there is a deep sense of reverence and gratitude towards the older generation in Asian cultures. In many cultures globally, families choose to care for their loved ones at home instead of relying on assisted living facilities. It's the cultural duty of younger family members to care for the elderly. In India, family leadership lies with the elders. Most times, they care for their grandchildren and help with the household chores. How do you think our society treats the elderly? Do we respect and honor our elders, or do we shun away from them? Are we patient enough to listen to their lessons or do we hide them away in nursing facilities? What comes to mind when you think of the term "old people"?

Psychologist Erik Erickson argued the Western fear of aging keeps us from living full lives. Some of our aged population are feeling they are losing value. We need to remember that elders have a wealth of experience and wisdom that are valuable assets that can be passed down to younger generations, helping them navigate life's challenges. We may discount them as old, frail, or perhaps foolish, but that is our prejudice. Although their bodies may lack health and their minds' sharpness fades, teachings abound if we listen. The death of an elder means losing their unique and vast knowledge unless we take the time to learn from them.

Individuals with disabilities can also serve as valuable teachers. Their spirit incarnated into a body to help us learn compassion. Challenges can be one of the highest form of soul evolution. What a spectacular selfless spirit to choose to incarnate with these lessons. The process of navigating challenges can lead to greater self-awareness, resilience, and personal transformation, ultimately contributing to one's soul evolution. Some individuals may unfairly judge people as being less capable or inferior due to their limitations. Let's embrace these individuals as valuable teachers who can inspire us with their courage, adaptability, and unique perspectives on life. One well-known teacher with disabilities was Steven Hawkins, one of the greatest scientists of his time. At age 21, doctors diagnosed him with ALS and didn't expect him to live another two years. Even from a wheelchair, unable to move or talk, he could give lectures after he developed a machine which allowed him to select words on a computer screen for synthesized speech. Interestingly, Dr. Hawkins gives credit to his disease for his accomplishments and talked about how it helped shape his life and purpose. He stated, "Before my condition was diagnosed, I had been very bored with life and there had not seemed to be anything worth doing." Interesting perspective, right? Our perception is that we possess infinite time and excellent health, however, our existence is fleeting. Life is indeed short. We have the choice to embrace our purpose and make a meaningful impact, or to extinguish our potential and remain passive in our journey.

Make it your goal to see people in their spiritual form instead of the human one. Why not experiment and greet everyone as spiritual beings? If we make spirit to spirit contact, we wouldn't just see disabilities or have preconceived ideas about anyone. We would just have the flow of love between hearts. We all have unique talents. Some people excel in one area, but face challenges in other areas. As we age, our control over our senses and mobility will gradually diminish. This loss of control can be challenging and may impact our overall well-being and quality of life. If you were in that scenario, what treatment would you prefer? Will we choose to age gracefully or be angry and bitter? We all face mortality, but the aim is to continue to be valuable and impactful to our family, friends, and community.

Children also teach us important lessons. They are closest to the Great Spirit with a childlike innocence of pure love and simplicity. Children laugh openly as they freely explore their surroundings, approaching each new situation with a sense of wonder. Our young ones have a natural ability to understand forgiveness. Imagine a world where forgiveness and laughter flow as swiftly as in children? How many of us carry hurt while children moved on from the situation? They effortlessly embrace the present moment and actively seek joy. They are the closest beings to Creator. Children see spirit easier than we can, and they don't force themselves to disregard their visions or imaginary friends. In fact, they seem to embrace it. They might tell you they spoke to grandma that just crossed over. They don't question, argue, rationalize, or deny spiritual happenings. Children possess a special kind of wisdom and spiritual intuition that allows them to see the world with wonder and curiosity, mirroring the divine nature of Creator. Be careful what you teach your children. Protect them from harmful programming for as long as you can. Mean behavior in children is taught and not a part of Creator. Why not remind them they are the little angels that walk among us? Reinforce positive behaviors and moral lessons. We are planting seeds in the minds and souls of children. Ask them what they think the tree is saying or have them listen to the plants or animals because they have the ability to hear them. Encourage their communication because all life is interconnected and we are only limited with what we are taught is impossible. Imagine if we break free of those barriers? We would be limitless — and we really are!

By opening our spirit to the surrounding lessons, we come to recognize that animals bring forth many teachings and healings. The depth of devotion and love that a pet exhibits is not often seen in human relationships. Is there anything better than a loyal pet waiting for you after a long day? They have no expectations, and they love you, warts and all. Animal friends are here to provide companionship and unconditional love. We owe them decent care for their existence in return. Our animal companions also know when to take action. There are countless stories of animals coming to the rescue of people. Consider the dolphin that rescued a boy who fell off a boat. The boy recounted a dolphin kept pushing him up to the surface throughout the night and prevented him from drowning until rescue workers arrived. We have relationships with all kinds of animals, including spiders and lizards. Animals do much more than provide us with a warm and fuzzy body. They help complete our emotional and spiritual needs as well. They are our spiritual companions that stay with us no matter if we are grumpy, mad, sad, or glad. Some are in tune with our very soul's essence and can heal us spiritually. How can anyone think of being cruel to animals? The four-legged ones can even embody human characteristics or a spirit reminiscent of a departed soul. Maybe there's something about your pet that feels familiar? However you want to explain it, our animals are intentionally put into our lives. Open up to the lessons they are providing. The animal life can open our hearts and help us feel peace. And when you feel at perfect peace, other animals can somehow sense it and start appearing to you. Wild animals will no longer fear you. Animals are intuitively aware of your silent communication with them. They have a unique understanding, and you'll soon realize your ability to connect with them. When you can do this, animal teachings will unfold.

Anna Breytenbach, a renowned wildlife communicator from South Africa, gained international recognition for her ability to connect with animals telepathically. One of her most well-known cases involved a black leopard named Diablo.[8] Diablo had spent most of his life in capacity and developed aggressive tendencies towards humans. Anna was brought in and, through her telepathic skills, was able to understand Diablo's traumas. Anna relayed his dissatisfaction with the darkness in his name and that he wanted respect for his true nature. He also misunderstood the safety and freedom available to him in his new enclosure. She relayed his message to the sanctuary owner, who changed his name to Spirit and fulfilled his other requests. Soon thereafter, he became a happy leopard. It's a heartwarming story and we encourage you to read the story. Anna is quite a fascinating, talented and giving person.

Let's remember that plants also have much to teach us and can serve as valuable teachers in our journey of understanding and connection with nature. They have the medicines they so willingly supply to us. It is their unspoken gift that they give freely for us to receive when we are in need. They also have a network of communication amongst themselves. Do you know that plants emit sound when in pain and send distress signals to each other? Mycelium is a fungus that expands underground and is often referred to as the "wood wide web," and is seen as a symbol of interconnectedness, cooperation, and unity in nature. When a tree is cut down, mycelium communicates to other trees, who care for the remaining trunk to try to save it. They feed it with water to protect it because the dying trunk is part of the forest family. Plant communication is part of a complex web, and some people are too arrogant to acknowledge their unique methods. Our existence is entangled in a mysterious web of life, still unexplored and misunderstood. Commit to removing blinders and embracing a broader perspective on life. Native people highly regard and honor plant people and their numerous roles. Plant people's spiritual energy balances life and is used for healing and prayers. Indigenous people see plants as family, not mere objects.

Rocks and minerals also have special healing abilities, and we can learn a lot from them as well. Catlinite, or Pipestone, is a natural stone located in the mines of the Minnesota's Pipestone National Monument. It is the sacred red clay stone that's traditionally used as a ceremony stone in Native American ceremonies. It is said that during the ancient times, the Great Spirit took the form of a large bird, stood upon a rock wall, and summoned all the tribes. After taking a red stone, he fashioned it into a pipe and smoked it. He said the red stone was their flesh, insisting it be solely used for pipe-making. Origin stories do differ among tribes, but the reverence with which the stories are passed down through generations is testimony to their importance.

We can't list all the teachers that encircle our web of life. But we ask that you focus on the accomplishments and gifts of those teachings versus the negativity that the media entangles us with. Kind and loving gestures often go unnoticed, contributing to widespread depression, stress, and anger. Numerous selfless individuals perform daily acts of kindness without desiring recognition. Look at volunteers donating precious time and money to those in need. There are so many angels among us. Treat everyone as if they could be angels, for you never truly know. Was there ever a time when someone's arrival blessed your life? It was like you were praying, and suddenly your prayer was answered. What a great gift!

Remember, you're a great teacher as well. Your inspirations are like seeds that will eventually bloom. Your kind words live on, even if they are not brought to your attention. Take, for example, a soldier who shared a story about losing his arm in an accident. Lying in the hospital bed, he contemplated a life without his arm. He was depressed and didn't know if he could move forward, but he remembered the encouraging words of his grade school gym teacher. That teacher expressed the belief he had the potential and capability to become a great school teacher. The former gym teacher's comment from years ago inspired the soldier to dedicate the rest of his life to teaching. The soldier expressed that his new teaching career was the biggest blessing in his life. One comment and one arm changed a man's life! By lifting others up with words of love and support, we have the ability to make a lasting and profound impact on their lives. Someone might not acknowledge that you made their day or gave them happy moments, but you have. Your words and actions hold immense power. We can't measure the impact, but they can evoke powerful feelings, and, as stated above, they can literally save a life. Even if you choose to only model negative behavior, you will still serve as a teacher in life. Your lesson will become a testament of what not to do or live by.

We can grow from negative situations as well. Have you ever had an experience where you learned a lesson from something you observed or happened in your life or the life of others? Perhaps you were raised in a family of alcoholics and vowed to never touch alcohol? Maybe you've experienced abuse or some other situation where you rose above it to become a resilient and compassionate person? There are so many situations that we would not choose for ourselves that are teachable moments. When we overcome these difficulties, it is our love and compassion that compels us to help others. This is how many nonprofit organizations are started. This is also why many volunteers do great things. Through their misfortune, their hearts reach out to help others. Occasionally, we must reassess our own position in life and discard unproductive teachings and behaviors not aligned with our original instructions. We must examine the accumulation of life lessons and evaluate how appropriate they are for our current situation. It might be time to release old behaviors and habits that limit our perspective on life. Perhaps these old habits and behaviors are ineffective, so it might be time to reframe your thinking. We will talk more about this in the chapter called removing blockages.

To summarize, teachings come in many forms. Look around you, there are teachers everywhere. From the blades of grass beneath our feet to the stars shining brightly above, they serve as our teachers. They are our elders, children, pets, challenging moments, and everything in-between. We need to stop, listen, honor, and give thanks to all our lessons. Reflect on the lessons you want to leave behind. What would your friends and loved ones say about you at your funeral? Every person has powerful lessons to share. There is an old saying that whenever a person dies, it is like burning down a library. Don't lose the lessons, open your spirit to them... learn and grow.

Larry's Aha Moment

I owned and operated a hair salon across the street from an archery store. David, the archery store owner, taught people how to shoot the bow, and he was a proud hunter. He loved to hunt the wild boar, and they are in abundance here in Texas. He'd guide people to top locations for pig hunts. He took around 75 people on a hunt 50 miles from Corpus Christi, spending the night with the group. Next day, he woke up late and rushed back in his Jeep to open the store. There was a pack of wild boars crossing the road, and his jeep clipped one of the pigs, and it flipped the jeep over. They found David and a pig lying side by side, dead. It was ironic that the one animal he preyed on and hunted most of his life ended up being responsible for his death.

When Native Americans hunt, we do it honorably, and we pray to allow the spirit of the animal to live on. Our intention is not to kill indiscriminately, unlike white men. Anytime you find a turtle shell, a feather or anything from animal life, whether it is dead or alive, we don't just take it. What we do is a tobacco offering, and we offer it to the four sacred directions because we don't know in what particular direction this animal had lived or which way its spirit may have gone. So we offer tobacco in the four sacred directions, and then we drop the tobacco right on the animal. We take just what is necessary. If you don't have tobacco, simply take the surrounding dirt with your left hand, as it is the most sacred side, closest to your heart.

One particular morning, when I was having my morning prayers, my heart was so opened. As I sat in a meditative state, the whitest of white doves appeared to me and was within arm's reach of my presence. It was not threatened by me. I took out my phone camera and took a picture to show to my wife. She mentioned that I just was visited by the Holy Spirit. Things like that happen when your heart is open. People, animals, and plants open up to you.

When I was at the Return of the Ancestors, David Swallow was singing a Wankan Tanka song and a song of thanks, and everyone was dancing, singing, and drumming, and eagles were flying in circles almost on top of the drums. It was such a blessing and beautiful sight. Eagles are the only birds that fly closest to Creator himself. It flies higher than any other bird. In our tradition, it is the one that carries our prayers to Creator. After my sister Pam and I completed our brother and sister ceremony, an eagle circled us about twenty-five feet above us to seal the deal and take our prayers to heaven. The circle is sacred to us. It is the circle of life and generations and the circle of four seasons. It has no beginning and no ending, so it is infinite.

There's a turtle story I want to tell you. As a vendor, I acquire turtle shells from various sources. Pam and I found these beautiful empty turtle shells around the lake where she lived, and I would bless them and make purses out of the larger ones and medicine bags out of the smaller ones. Once, I was at a market in San Angelo and saw two macho guys standing there. I was at my booth sewing a shirt together when one guy wanted to tell me a story. I stopped what I was doing and listened. I was told that a few days earlier, they were at their stock pond, where they saw many turtles were eating the newly stocked fish. So he went out and bought a case of beer and several boxes of .22 shells. He and his friend sat there drinking beer, head- popping all these turtles, and it was a killing field of all these turtles. I was just listening to this story in disgust. After he finished, I mentioned the same thing happening to our buffalo in the past. The young man apologized to me, but I said to him, "Yeah, but who is going to apologize to the turtles?" He said he never thought about it that way and left in shame, and with a better understanding of how Native people feel and not to shoot things just because there is an abundance of animals around.

Pam's Aha Moment

Many animals come into my waking world and my dream world to give me teachings or to ask for help. In my younger years, the wolf continued to appear in my dreams, and I've even dreamt of being a wolf to protect people. I've had dreams where large eagles land at the water's edge with an injury, and they ask me for help and to protect them from humans. I even swam with dolphins that brought me to another realm to listen to the "one" dolphin who lectured about love. I seem to understand animals better than humans and I think many of you reading this right now can relate. There is no pretense, hidden agendas, or deception with animals. They freely give their love and have many lessons to teach us if we choose to listen.

Over twenty-five years ago, I experienced a divorce, and the process was painful and lonely. One particular day, I prayed to my deceased brother, asking for help during this difficult transition. I asked him for a sign to know he was with me. That night, we were going to experience a freeze and my friend called and advised me to drip water on the dock to prevent my pipes from bursting. Despite my reluctance, I found the energy to go out and turn on the water. As I reached down to open the faucet, I heard a sound in the water, like someone blowing bubbles. A baby dolphin was in the canal! It was quite rare to have one swim in the small canals, yet there he was, blowing air right onto my hand. I thought it was as if my brother came down and said, "It's going to be okay." That was my sign, and that was the day I started to heal. To this day, dolphins remind me to be alive, joyful, and playful.

There was a young reverend who had a stroke and was a patient in the nursing home where I worked. He couldn't talk coherently, but he was one of our favorites because he was always smiling and had such an easygoing and loving spirit about him. He had that special something that we all adored. One day, his wife approached me, praising his community contributions and questioning why God allowed this to happen, as he had much to teach. I told her what was in my heart. He was still teaching. He was teaching us all to be compassionate and patient every day. He was joyful, despite the medical condition he had. He made me feel an abundance of love. When I worked in the nursing home, I learned many lessons. I saw the challenges of surrendering control and permitting someone else to assume responsibility for one's care. My heart went out to them. Some patients also expressed regrets. If given another chance, they said they would have taken more risks and embrace life's opportunities. The lesson has stayed with me, serving as a reminder to live fully and embrace all the ups and downs on my Red Road journey.

CEREMONIES

There are times we travel to the remote corners of the earth or we climb the top of a mountain to witness a beautiful or sacred site; we are in ceremony. When we attend certain events in our lives or partake in religious services; we are in ceremony. All cultures have ceremonies. Taking part in ceremonies boils down to your intent. Showering can be a ceremony when intended, whereas attending church without an open heart may not be a ceremony if you are just going through the motions. Ceremony is a way of connecting to spirit, but it also challenges you to surrender. When Jesus broke bread and gave it to the disciples, he said, "This is my body given for you." So it was not just a ritual, it was bringing Christ into their hearts. Ceremony is much more than being there. It is taking spirit into your form.

Formal ceremonies can be awe-inspiring and glamorous, but it can also be as simple as taking in your breath. Anyone can take a minute or two in their busy lives to focus on their breathing. Being aware of your breath relaxes the mind, body, and soul. Inhaling and exhaling can become a ceremony. Try it. Find a quiet spot, sit, and focus on your breath going in and out. Feel the air go into your nose, into your lungs, and out again. Do this slowly and deeply. Inhale through your nose and tell yourself to relax, love, and find peace. Any mantra will work. Exhale through your mouth, releasing what you no longer wish to hold on to. Breathe out stress, negativity, or any tightness you may feel in your body. For example, you can say to yourself, "Breathe in peace and breathe out stress." When you are breathing, it is normal for thoughts to pop into your head. If a thought arises, label it as such. Silently say "thought" and then shift your attention back to your breathing. At the beginning of your breathing practice, you might have countless thoughts. We are not used to shutting down our conscious mind, it's always chattering. When you want it to be quiet, like trying to sleep, your mind keeps ruminating on the day's events. So this will take practice. But it is a simple ceremony you can take with you wherever or whatever you are doing. We need the air we breathe to survive, so air is a miracle in itself. When you wake up in the morning, start your day with a breathing ceremony. Waking up in the morning and breathing in gratitude is a perfect ceremony. Walking can also be a ceremony because every step we take is sacred. Thich Nhat Hanh says that when you practice walking meditation in a relaxed, peaceful way; you step not only for ourselves but for the world. We see we are all linked both in suffering and happiness.9

The breath of life is our first ceremony. It is often used as a way to honor and give thanks for the gift of life, to clear stagnant energy, and to connect with the spiritual realm. It is also used in healing ceremonies to restore balance and harmony to the body and spirit. Participants in the breath of life ceremony often gather in a circle, breathing together in rhythm with the beat of the drum and chanting of sacred songs. We also have a breathing ceremony called "taking in the air," or "wind ceremony". When we see an animal struck by a car on the side of the road and it is at the last stages of dying; we do a ceremony. We cup our hands like we are going to shout out and bring it to the animal's nose, and we suck up the air from his nostrils to our lungs. In this way, you inhale the air to combine its last breath with yours. Then later, when you are doing your prayers, you are releasing the animal in your prayers. Without breath, all life ceases. Understand that animals, plants, and even rocks breath. The winds breathe. There are so many ceremonies that Native Americans perform. To learn more, one book I would recommend is *Mother Earth Spirituality*10 by Ed McGaa Eagle Man. This book has good energy and further explains Native American spirituality and ceremonies.

We should strive to maintain a constant state of ceremony. Witnessing a baby bird hatching in a nest is a miraculous event. When a baby is born, it is a miracle of life. In ceremonies, giving thanks informs the spirit people of your gratitude for their gifts. Native people do corn pollen and tobacco ceremonies where we pinch a little of it with our fingers and we offer it to the four sacred directions. We drop the pollen or tobacco in the four sacred directions to give thanks. The four sacred directions are east, south, west and north. Creator (Christ) is the fifth sacred direction (up), Mother Earth is the sixth (down), and your heart is the seventh (inward). We consider everything else before we consider ourselves; that is just what Native People do.

When facing each direction, draw energy in from that corner of the earth.

East—facing east means embracing new beginnings, the sunrise, and the birth of a new day. You thank all the people and Wisdom Keepers from the east.

South—when facing south, it's the source of harvest, growth, and ancient wisdom. We gain wisdom from our predecessors.

West—the source of all teachings. The wisdom comes in through the west, where we receive a lot of our ceremonies from.

North—the corner of the earth that gives us strength. It teaches us to be strong, to endure, and it brings in purity, cleansing.

UP—when you look up to spirit, you receive love and teachings.

Down—when you look down and touch Mother Earth, physically touch her with your bare feet, you are connecting to Mother Earth and receiving everything she offers.

Inward—when you touch your own heart, seventh direction, it means you are okay with everything that is being given to you. You love yourself and are becoming a provider for everyone else, so you consider yourself as well for protection, love, and nurturing.

These are the directions we pray to daily. We perform many other ceremonies. To learn more, research and consult your elders. Please remember that expressing gratitude is a significant ceremonial practice for us. Through the practice of gratitude ceremonies, individuals are reminded of their place in the greater web of life and their responsibility to honor and protect the gifts they have been given.

Drums are an important part of Native American ceremonies. Nations worldwide use drums. All cultures possess drums of various types. We are drawn to the drum for a reason, a purpose. It reminds us when we were in mother's womb, when we were nestled close to her heart. The beat of the music reminds us of her, and the beat and its rhythm are healing. When a child needs comforting and a mother picks the child up, she puts her right next to her bosom and the baby is satisfied. Why? Because the baby hears the heartbeat. We even have machines we put in babies' cribs to comfort the child to sleep. If you think about it, your heartbeat is your own drum. When you sit quietly and look at a beautiful sunrise or sunset, feel the pulse of your heartbeat. Connecting with Mother Earth requires no special efforts. She is all around you. Listen to her pulse, listen to her song. People from various backgrounds gather at our Corpus drum circle, seeking healing. Whether it is physical, emotional, or spiritual doesn't matter. Your heartbeat can become your drum if you don't have one with you. You already have a drum within yourself.

The sacred "pipe" ceremony holds significance among Native Americans. The pipe has been around since the White Buffalo Calf Woman brought it to us to connect with Creator, to connect with nature, to connect with other people's spirit, to connect us to the spirit world, and to connect us with our ancestors. When you connect the pipe together with the bowl and the stem, you are connecting both male and female—you are connecting Mother Earth to God. You are asking Creator to step forward to be with you. The pipes have to keep ongoing. Remember, this Indian artifact deserves genuine appreciation, not mere display. It is a living, breathing thing that needs to be kept alive and honored. Like the Bible, some people keep it hidden in a book cabinet. But the Bible is intended to be read, meant to be used. The pipe is the same way. When we unite the pipe, we ask these entities to be present, sharing in the moment of our lightness and prayers. Truth prevails when the pipe is assembled. Spirit is there at the peak, ready to answer and help, regardless of the number of people. Our people have conducted the pipe ceremony for thousands of years, aligning with our traditions. It is historically and religiously correct. It records our time, efforts, suffering, and binds us together. Years of attempts to take our pipe ceremony forced us to hide it. We secretly upheld our cherished traditions at night or in secluded locations. They stripped us away from our Native culture and rewrote history to change it to fit their needs. They have taken away our land, our culture, our religion, even the bones of our ancestors, but one thing they could never take away from us is our ways on how to pray with the sacred pipe. We don't allow anyone to take pictures when the pipe ceremony is being conducted. Your personal time and connection with the Great Spirit should remain private and not be publicized or flaunted. The pipe is used for personal connection and prayer time with Creator. It is powerful to all nations, and it is what connects us to Mother Earth, the star people, and Christ himself.

A simple ceremony you can do with the pipe is a personal pipe ceremony where you just load it up yourself and you smoke it yourself. We don't inhale when we draw from the pipe. We hold it in our mouth, and when we say our prayer, we let our prayer out with the smoke. No scent reaches higher than tobacco. It is the one plant that the root grows deep, deep into Mother Earth. It is connected to me, and it is connected to the heavens. The ceremony must be done properly. Tobacco is the richest products the Native Americans have to use for prayer. Everyone thinks tobacco should be used for consumption, but it wasn't designed that way. It was designed to be used as an offering, a prayer. You shred the leaf, and you grab a little with your left hand. Your left side being your most sacred side, the side closest to your heart, and you offer tobacco to the four sacred directions — that alone is a ceremony. Tobacco should always be considered as a ceremony, not inhaling into your lungs. It wasn't meant for that. When our people were imprisoned and they didn't have their pipes or tobacco, they would use dirt to conduct their private ceremonies. Ceremonies were that important to them.

There are countless number of Indigenous ceremonies that have specific spiritual purpose, from healing to gratitude. We discussed briefly the pipe ceremony but there are myriad of other ceremonies. It is vital for readers to grasp that these ceremonies encompass much more than just dancing and singing. They always include connection to spirit and creator. The Sweat Lodge/Inipi Ceremony is practiced by many First Nations people. It can be practiced alone or before or after different ceremonies. It is meant to be cleansing/purifying physically, emotionally, and spiritually. Every part of the sweat lodge ceremony is a prayer, an offering to the Great Spirit. It is a purification ritual where community members cleanse through sweat as a symbol of surrender and a form of offering. It is acknowledging a sacred connection with all relatives. Aho Mitakuye Oyasın. We are all related.

Ceremonies still have a specific purpose for Indian people. To be fortunate enough to participate in sacred ceremonies is an honor. But please understand and follow the rules of the person/tribe conducting the ceremony. Each ceremony can be performed differently, and many are based on a particular story passed on by elders, holy people, or their origin story. Indigenous cultures did not have a bible or book for reference. They relied on the elders to teach and keep the ceremonies alive. Therefore, it is important for everyone to understand that ceremonial ways can vary based on differing histories and beliefs. We have witnessed people contradicting the ways a particular ceremony is performed, and this is not the teachings of the Red Road.

For example, in the book *Breath of the Invisible*, John Redtail Freesoul teaches us that the sacred pipe was brought to different tribes through different messengers. To the Blackfoot it was Thunder, to the Arapahoe it was Duck. To many tribes, it was White Buffalo Calf Maiden. It was the prophet Sweet Medicine who brought the arrow pipe bundle to the Cheyennes. In our hearts, we must recognize that native people's universal message is the connection to Creator and spirit in all of creation. Everything you see, hear or touch has a message or lesson, even the rocks are alive. These ceremonies increase our communion with spirit and when we do, everything becomes alive. By doing this, we can better understand the messages from the animals, plants, and minerals. During a sweat ceremony, we commonly say "Mitakuye Oyasin" to all our relations. From the Lakota language, it embodies interconnectedness. It is a prayer of oneness and harmony with all forms of life: other people, animals, birds, insects, trees and plants, and even rocks, rivers, mountains and valleys.11

There are countless Indigenous ceremonies. Some include, Birthing, Coming of Age, Solstice, Medicine, Naming, Wedding, Sunrise, End of Life, Full Moon, Potlatch, Pow Wow, Healing, Sundance, Vision Quest, Talking Stick, Hunting, Sweat Lodge, to name a few. Smudging is a sacred practice that has been used by Native Americans for centuries. It involves burning sage, cedar and/or sweetgrass, to purify the body, mind and spirit. It is done before many traditional ceremonies and rituals. Smudging is used to connect with the spirit world and it also seeks guidance and protection. It carries prayers and intentions up to Creator. It is important in many healing ceremonies because of the cleansing properties that help remove negative energy and restore balance. Returning to a circle requires smudging each time. We use sage with our morning prayers and when we write spiritual messages (this book in particular) to ask for guidance from Creator.

When Pamela Two Spirits and I had our brother and sister ceremony, it was done in a sacred manner. We were in constant prayer, and the drum was beating while a sacred fire was lit. We gave thanks to the four sacred directions, Creator, Mother Earth, as we spoke of our new relations. We smoked the pipe in a sacred way, and we cut our hands and bonded them in leather. This ceremony holds great significance, as it officially makes us siblings. When we speak of one another, we speak as brother and sister. This is a lifelong commitment to be honored and held in deep regard.

Cleansing and renewing your spirit is also a type of ceremony you do for yourself. People may attend a seminar or go on vacation or sabbatical to renew their spirit. It doesn't matter what you do. Occasionally, we must renew and cleanse our spirit. Choices range from sweat lodges and retreats to lectures and long walks. It is being in the quiet moments where you are not rushed or stressed. Cleansing is a very important ceremony for our people. Every day, we smudge ourselves when we leave our house. By doing so, we protect ourselves from negativity and toxins when we venture out into the world. When we come back home, we re-cleanse by smudging again, so you rid yourself of all that. Even taking a hot shower is a form of cleansing. Our people enter sweat lodges to cleanse and rejuvenate ourselves. The sweat lodge represents the belly of Mother Earth. There are rocks, and when you pour water on the rocks, it gives off steam and you sweat. What you are doing is sweating out your impurities, detoxifying yourself from everything inside you. When you emerge, you're reborn, starting anew. You are being reborn through the belly of Mother Earth. When we go to the sweat lodges, we usually go in buck naked, and we go out buck naked as if we are being reborn. So that is a feminine aspect and how we revere our women. Native Americans also have peyote ceremonies and we go on vision quests. We do a lot of nature's ways of cleaning ourselves. We always try to keep a cleansed body physically, mentally, and spiritually. We try to rid ourselves of our toxins that we carry deep inside, knowing that we carry stress until it manifests physically. It is unlimited what stress can do. Eventually, it is going to come out if you repress stress.

There are many ways to perform ceremonies. It can be as simple as lighting a candle, reading the bible or other sacred or inspirational book. It can be attending a particular church, synagogue, Buddhist Temple, or Mosque. Maybe you have a spiritual area in your house where you keep things dear to your heart. Consider lighting sage or a candle to remember someone or to send a special thought or prayer. Ceremonies are not bound by a specific model. Rather, it is all about your intent. Without access to native ceremonies, many alternatives are available in the new age market. There are sound baths, meditation, yoga, massage, fire, breathing, dancing, just to name a few. It can be as simple as praying over your meal or saying thank you to a sunrise or sunset. That's ceremony right there. Upon waking, think of things you're grateful for before any other thoughts arise. Make a habit of saying a gratitude prayer. Commit fully with your heart and soul. Absorb and embody the teachings and spirit of the message. Find a ceremony that you resonate with and practice daily. It can be as simple as the breathing exercise we discuss in this chapter. Who can judge your ceremony as wrong if it is loving and kind? We want to make a point that we do not judge others' ceremonies or ways. Natives faced severe judgment and look at the outcome. Wars persist as we assert our righteousness over their wrongness. Let's practice Creator's number one lesson. Love one another.

Ishka
    Larry Running Turtle Salazar

AUTHENTIC LIVING

W*isdom comes only when you stop looking for it and start living the life the creator intended for you.*
— Hopi

Listen to the wind, it talks. Listen to the silence, it speaks, listen to your heart, it knows.
— Native American proverb

Authentic living is connecting with our soul's purpose. It is embodying one's true essence and values in all aspects of life, while maintaining a deep connection to Creator, and our inner wisdom. Authentic living leads to a greater sense of fulfillment, connection, and harmony with oneself, others, and the world. Our waking world and our dreams often provide subtle but powerful signs that affirm and validate the direction we are meant to take on our Red Road journey. Paying attention to these signs and trusting in their guidance helps us find clarity, alignment, and fulfillment in our chosen path. Spirit is always communicating with us, whether or not we're listening. Messages from the spiritual realm can come in various forms, such as intuition, synchronicities, dreams, and physical sensations. It is up to us to cultivate a practice of mindfulness, openness, and receptivity in order to tune into these subtle messages and guidance.

It's important not to allow the opinions or expectations of others to influence your soul's purpose. Other people do not know what your soul is designed for. Seeking validation or guidance from others may lead you astray from your true path. Your true purpose comes from within. Align with your authentic self and listen to the whispers of your soul — uncover the essence of who you are and what you are meant to contribute to the world. If you listen deep inside yourself, you will awaken. Our thoughts and beliefs can sometimes overpower the voice of our heart and confuse our journey. Our ego tries to distract us from authenticity and it can keep us stuck in drama, trapped in our head with worrying thoughts. Worrying is like praying for something you don't want. Continuously dwelling on a problem only serves to manifest something negative instead of focusing on positive outcomes. Living authentically becomes challenging when we place more importance on our ego, external influences, and societal expectations. This process drains our inner energy and shifts it toward the external world. It closes the door to our heart and allows our mind to become dominate. That behavior stops the normal ebb and flow of resonating with what we intuitively know. Like a programmed computer, our mind analyzes and presents detailed consequences of our thoughts and actions. Our mind thinks it is protecting us, but the truth is quite the opposite. It can block us from our creative thought process and the voice of spirit. We will discuss how to change your mental programing in later chapters called, 'Removing Blockages & Manifesting'.

The ego does provide some benefits, such as promoting individuality and self-preservation, maintaining one's identity and sense of self. It helps to navigate social and societal norms. But ego can hinder authentic living by creating a false sense of self-importance, promoting selfish desires and materialistic pursuits. It can fuel fear and insecurity and disconnect you from genuine emotions and relationships. This can lead to a lack of fulfillment and inner conflict, preventing you from living in alignment with your true values and purpose. It is time to listen beyond your senses without interference from your strong and overpowering egos. It is learning to slow down not only your physical bodies but also your thoughts as well. The ego traps us in the past and future. It does not exist in the now. It attempts to confine and categorize us, keeping us caught in the cycle of conflict and separation. The Ego preoccupies itself with survival, identity, and success. Anything that is drama and divisive is ego driven. Eckhart Tolle describes ego in his book, *A New Earth*: "An ego that wants something from another — and what ego doesn't — will play some kind of role to get its 'needs' met, be they material gain, a sense of power, superiority, or specialness, or some kind of gratification, be it physical or psychological. People are unaware of the roles they play. They are those roles. Some roles are subtle; others are obvious, except to the person playing it. Some roles have the sole purpose of getting attention from others. The ego thrives on others' attention...such as recognition, praise, admiration, or just to be noticed to have its existence acknowledged."12

Recall a time when your actions resonated deeply with your essence, rather than being motivated by ego. It was a knowing, a silent communication between you and your soul that you were in perfect harmony. Take a minute and try to recall that memory. The opposite is also true. Have you ever gone against your instincts and followed through with something, anyway? We all have at least one stupid incident where we could kick ourselves because we knew what the outcome would be. But remember, no one is perfect. If one day is unsuccessful, there's always another day. When you become aware, that is the first step in awakening to your soul's purpose.

Once aware of your true identity, being is all that matters. You feel neither superior to anyone nor inferior to anyone, and you have no need for approval because you've awakened to your own infinite worth.
— Deepak Chopra

Being authentic means aligning to what resonates with you. Many well-intentioned individuals advise us on how to live, but if it doesn't align with your inner wisdom, it's not for you. How do they know your soul's purpose? Walt Disney is a good example of a person staying authentic. Inspired by his imagination, he was guided towards the journey of exploring his creativity. It may come as a surprise, but Walt Disney was actually fired from a job because they considered him uncreative. Imagine if he believed them? And do you remember the book, "The Cat in the Hat"? Twenty-seven different publishers rejected the author's first book. These are two great examples of individuals who followed their inner sense of purpose and persevered in their journey despite facing criticism and setbacks. Embracing authenticity is a valuable privilege that plays a significant role in our personal growth and evolution. Imagine a garden filled with all the same colored flowers? Every living thing in the vast tapestry of existence holds a unique purpose, continuously exploring and expanding in the interconnected web of all that is. Each individual, no matter how small or seemingly insignificant, plays a vital part in the harmonious balance of nature. Your profession could range from being a gardener at a small nursery to holding the position of a CEO in a major corporation. It's what sings to your heart that matters. We are not advocating to quit your job, give up all your possessions, and search for your inner purpose. Sensible actions are necessary for basic needs like money and shelter. That being said, your purpose should not be primarily about monetary gain. Money is useful, and we all like it, but money doesn't buy happiness. If you choose to go into a profession because of money and not your love for the job, you won't be aligned to your soul's purpose. Yes, outwardly, people with money, power, and big egos are in the spotlight and live bigger lives, but that is the outer appearances and may not represent accurate inner peace, joy, and happiness. If money can buy happiness, why do some celebrities use drugs and alcohol? Why do they experience depression? Why do they commit suicide?

The desire for more is deeply rooted in society and it distracts us from living in a way that is true to ourselves. This can create a sense of disconnection from our authentic selves and a constant state of seeking fulfillment outside ourselves. Television and magazines inundate us with images of happy people with new things, but that is an illusion. Have you ever observed a small child playing with the box that a toy came from? Small children are unaware and uninterested in the price of items. What led us to become a materialistic society? What is the reason we need immediate gratification? It's a societal expectation that we should have the newest and best things, and that we deserve them. Companies spend millions of dollars marketing and programming us to think that we need the latest gadgets; making us believe we can't be happy without them. If you are authentically happy and have love in your heart, you don't need more stuff. You realize the stuff you need is already within you. We've all experienced the "I want" phase, but if you reflect on happy memories, it's rarely about material possessions. It is usually a special moment, perhaps a laugh, or something you shared with a loved one. It's usually a simple moment or encounter with a person who warms your heart. Activities like fishing, walking, bird-watching, gardening, etc. are simple yet fulfilling. Chasing material possessions because we feel our family needs more is an illusion. Our children do not need more stuff; they need guidance, attention, love, and our time. We are not encouraging a mindset of being overly frugal or denying oneself of nice things. Our advocacy is for a balanced and content life, living within your means. Our job is to guide our children to pursue their passions. What are you teaching your children? Are you teaching them competition, the need for more, chaos, and drama? You are their greatest role model and they have eyes and ears that record everything you say and do. When you are insecure, stressed, busy, and out of balance, you model that for your children. They won't say it out loud, but they absorb the lesson. Teach them how to honor themselves. Teach them to listen to the butterfly, to watch a cloud, sing a song, or plant and harvest a garden.

To live authentically, we must also limit our preoccupation with body image. Despite our diverse forms, we are rarely satisfied with our own. When will society realize that our outer shell is not as important as our inner one? Our body is only temporary, and it ages and dies — period. Only our soul moves on. Yet society inundates us with constant messages and products that claim to be necessary for a better life. We go to great lengths and spend a lot of money, believing this to be true. Look at the billions of dollars spent on weight loss alone. A lot of effort goes into outward appearances. When we put all our attention and focus on our body, it becomes the center of our reality. When our body image consumes us, we are disconnected from our true essence, leading to an imbalance of spiritual growth. We forget we are spirit having a human experience. Connect with your heart, passion, and soul, and you will become light and open. You will become more empathetic, heartfelt, grateful, compassionate, and interconnected. When you connect to who you really are, your soul can journey. Imagine the possibilities if we dedicated equal time and effort to nurturing both our physical and spiritual well-being? If you spend an hour getting dressed in the morning, slot an hour for your spiritual growth. Are you willing to take that challenge?

We have all experienced insecurities and fear in our lives. Escaping all fears is impossible, and some fear is necessary. However, if you focus mainly on insecurity and fear, it will immobilize the process of authentic living before it can even start. When you begin the exploration process of brainstorming your journey, don't let negativity stop the creative process. Negativity is like a stop sign. It obstructs ideas from coming to you. How can ideas present themselves if you're always stopping them? Fear can create uncertainty and indecision, hindering the progress and stopping you from potentially groundbreaking ideas. Remember that fear is the opposite of love. Focus on reducing fear by breathing in love and breathing out fear every day until you feel relaxed or less anxious. When you are relaxed, you are a better decision maker. It's normal to feel anxious about starting a new project or a journey. Refocus your perspective—think of it as anticipation masked as nervousness. Feeling nervous about starting a new job or doing something for the first time is normal. Recall the moment when you first rode your bike. Were you a pro on your first try? Probably not. I'll bet football players had years of honing their practice before they became pros. All things improve with time and practice.

Living authentically is easier when you quiet your emotional drama. Emotions are a natural aspect of our humanity, and it is important to acknowledge and appreciate them for the insights they provide. For instance, our anger stems from hurt, so when we feel anger, we must nurture ourselves. How would we respond to a hurt child? We might give them a hug and tell them we're sorry they're hurting. Apply the same principle to yourself to help you release anger. Don't get sucked into staying angry or in drama. Ask yourself what is your anger teaching you and then move on. Don't hang on to it. After you experience any emotional drama, ask yourself if your current situation is leading you on the Good Red Road. If the answer is no, release it. We can all think of that one person in our lives that everything they touch is drama, drama, drama, and they seem to thrive on that energy. They don't see the forest for the trees.They skip along, seemingly recharging themselves from one drama scene to the next. Even the term drama queen is recognized and sometimes even promoted in our society. When trapped in this cycle, it's like a hamster on a spinning wheel. These dramatic situations may give people a temporary high, but it's not authentic living. To live authentically, you must learn to quiet down your physical and emotional self, open your hearts, and let go of drama. Here is a Zen story about letting go. Tanzan and Ekido were two monks traveling together down a muddy road. A heavy rain was falling. Walking around a bend, they met a girl in a silk kimono. She was unable to cross the muddy road because it would ruin her dress. "Come," Tanzan said, immediately lifting her, carrying her over the mud, and setting her down across the road. The monks pressed forward, and Ekido remained silent until they neared the temple. "We monks are not supposed to touch females. Why did you do that?" Ekido asked. "I put the girl down hours ago," said Tanzan. "Why are you still carrying her?" This story shows how we carry unnecessary pain without cause. Release the pain.

When your thoughts move toward negative stories, you can simply say "drama" and stop the continued negative thought process. Stop this unproductive habit. What if it is not your drama but another person's? Imagine it as a radio. You have the power to turn down the volume or change channels. If you don't like what you are hearing, simply change the subject or leave. Drama brings you further and further from your spiritual self. It zaps your energy, lowers your vibration, and you end up feeling like a wet facecloth. Run, don't walk, to the nearest exit! You hold the power to cease replaying and engaging in negative emotions and others' drama.

Our society places a high importance on conformity. This story exemplifies that. A story unfolds as an old man, a little boy, and a donkey walking to a city. They passed through several small villages along the way. At the first village, they heard people whispering and laughing. Some said it was dumb to walk when there was a perfectly good donkey to ride. The man pondered and agreed. So he put the little boy on the donkey, and he walked beside them. Upon reaching the next village, whispers and laughter greet them. He heard them say what a disrespecting little boy who rode while the old man walked. After considering, the old man agrees to let the little boy walk while he rode the donkey. Nearby villagers laughed and pointed at the old man riding while the little boy walked. The old man decided they will both ride the donkey. When they reach the next town, villagers point and whisper about the poor donkey carrying two people and how it was terrible to treat an animal like that. So they end up carrying the donkey into the city. Does this story reflect your life? Are you living your life according to others in order to fit in? If you are, then you are not living authentically. If you let others' laughter shape you, you're not being true to yourself. People will always talk, regardless of your choices. No matter your actions or lifestyle, it's impossible to please everyone, and the same goes for others pleasing you. Grant others the freedom to speak and live as they choose. We all have our own lessons to learn.

Say this mantra out loud: "My life lesson is not their life lesson. His life lesson is not my life lesson. Her life lesson is not my life lesson." Earth is a one big school, and we all have different lessons. We can't all be aligned on the same physical, emotional, or spiritual path. Our spirit is interconnected to all things. However, we have different ways of living our lives. We are interconnected, yet as individuals, we have different journeys. Our goal is to walk the Good Red Road's spiritual path, embodying loving principles. However, each individual will have a different approach to achieve this. If you are walking the Good Red Road, you are awakening to the fact that we are all interconnected; and you are awakening to loving and honoring yourself, your brothers and sisters, and all life. You are listening to spirit that is within and all around you. Your heart is open and you realize that you are spirit having a human experience. Spirit is with you, a part of you, and everything else. You listen to the voices and messages that present themselves to you. When you align yourself to these principles, your journey presents itself to you. It magically unfolds. When you awaken, you understand that no task is too big or small for you to conquer. The sky is the limit when you are authentic!

Dream-inspired discoveries, creativities, and inventions also tap into your soul's purpose. For example, Beethoven dreamt of some of his piano sonatas, and Paul McCartney dreamt of the tune to the song "Yesterday." Dreams can be a form of communication from your soul.

Perhaps you have had a problem solved after you've "slept" on it. Awaken to your dream or meditative state and see what it is trying to communicate. Don't jump out of your bed as soon as you wake up. Quiet your mind for that first few moments and try to recall your dreams. Don't worry if you can't right away. Like anything else, it takes practice. It's also a good time to ask your guides and Creator to speak to you. Your mind will be calm, and it's easier for spirit to come through. This is a good time to ask, "What is my purpose? What resonates with me?" Don't force the answers, just allow the messages to unfold. They might come in images or bits and pieces of information, but that is okay. Once you start recognizing messages, they will get stronger and louder. This technique can be practiced every morning with your daily affirmation. Every day, state your focus. For example, before you get out of bed, you can say, "Today I am going to slow down." It is not enough agreeing with some of these principles we talk about in this book. Start integrating them into your life by taking small, measurable steps to make them a part of your journey.

In summary, living authentically helps you realize your purpose. Listen with your heart, slow down, and open up to the miracles all around you. Secrets whisper all around us. Listen not only with your ears, but with your soul. Remember that every two-and four-legged has a purpose. Father Sky, Grandmother Moon, Mother Earth — all have purpose. The winged ones — plants, rocks, and trees — all have purpose. Find your soul's purpose. Ask Creator and spirit to help guide you. Have ceremony in the morning to align yourself for your day's journey. Doing so sets your mind, body, and soul in harmonious alignment. We leave you with the knowledge that every step you take is sacred.

Larry's Aha Moment

When I moved to Corpus Christi in 1962, I enrolled in school, but I couldn't be Native. They took away all my authenticity, and I only became myself when I got home from school and my mom taught me the Native ways. I was caught between two worlds, and I've always felt that way. My true life lies in the wilderness, nature, and ceremonies. My pretend life is what everybody else wants to see in me. A lot of times I bring forth my authentic life to my real world and that attracts certain people to me, but I have to keep a separation in order to keep my sanity. My real world is a constant hustle and bustle, full of cell phones, computers, and everything related to connecting with the world. I fight battles and laws, continuously advocating for our people. Our weapons of choice are now our cell phones, briefcases, and I have to live the hustle and bustle life to keep our culture alive. However, my authentic life is when I come home and I work on my hides and I'm making drums and working on teaching my children and nephews the Native culture. That is my authentic self right there. That is when I get lost within myself in my own authenticity, in my own culture. I love to be amongst the trees and nature. I inform city dwellers of my journey to see my sister Pamela Two Spirits. I told the people who were asking me where I was going. I told them that I was on my way to visit my relatives — the trees, the lakes, the rocks, the fish — and that they touch my spirit in ways that my human relatives don't. These relatives I am visiting, is how my ancestors learned about life.

Pam's Aha Moments

I understand how tough it is to know who you are. I struggled because I felt different and alone. My dream visions helped me understand interconnectedness, but I still didn't fully grasp why this was happening. It wasn't until I became a hospice nurse that I finally merged and understood my dream visions and purpose. I believe we are all one and interconnected, yet we are here to learn our individual lessons. We can help each other on the journey by loving; not judging. Our primary soul lesson is to love. But I have to be honest. Some of the lessons are like "WOW" and other lessons are like "OH CRAP NOT AGAIN". We are all here to evolve, but remember...no matter where you are right now in your journey, never give up or forget to be kind and true to yourself. Find your passion and let your heart sing. Publishing this book with Larry is my soul's purpose. I want our words of encouragement from our soul to resonate with yours. My hope is this book will help you understand that you are loved no matter what!

MINDFULNESS OR MONKEY MIND

T raining began with children who were taught to sit still and enjoy it. They were taught to use their organs of smell, to look when there was apparently nothing to see, to listen intently when all was seemingly quiet.
— Luther Standing Bear

Life is what happens when you are making other plans. — John Lennon

Overthinking can make it difficult to be in the present moment. When our minds are wandering in thought, unaware of our surroundings, we may overlook valuable experiences. We live in our thoughts while we walk, talk, eat, shop, or perform any activity. If you observe your surroundings, you may notice people with distant, blank expressions, as if they are lost in space. Or, they may be constantly on their phones, talking, scrolling or texting. We've all seen entertaining videos that show people falling into water or walking into walls while engrossed with their phones. We laugh and shake our head, but we're also distracted by our phones. Reflect on a time you were alone in a store. Did you find yourself distracted by a phone conversation, or perhaps you were lost in thought, oblivious to your surroundings? We understand that challenge being trapped in past or future thinking. Being in the presence moment takes practice. Next time you are shopping, focus on being mindful. As you walk through the aisles, focus on your senses by noticing colors, textures and the surrounding smells. Pay attention to the sounds of people chatting and the checkout beeping. You can practice mindful breathing by focusing on your breath and noticing the sensation of air entering and leaving your body. These techniques can help bring your attention back to the present moment. Exercises that you can practice at home include progressive muscle relaxation, gratitude practice, engaging your senses, journaling, walking in nature, yoga, meditation, to name a few. There are grounding techniques you can use to anchor yourself in the present moment, such as feeling the ground beneath your feet, listening to sounds around you, or feeling the wind against your face. There are many techniques available — search for one that resonates with you.

Learning to be mindful is difficult because we face bombardment from every imaginable source of stimuli. We watch TV, listen to the radio, receive and deliver phone and text messages, scroll news feeds and social media. We receive too much input and become overly stimulated. It can feel as though our mind is tuning into multiple radio stations simultaneously. Even when we try to sleep, our conscious mind remains active and we have difficulty sleeping. Our mind chatters incessantly like a monkey. According to Buddhist principles, monkey mind is a term that refers to being unsettled. It's the part of our brain most connected with the ego and it takes a lot of self-control to quiet the monkey.

Shifting from your thoughts to being present takes awareness and practice. In his book, *A New Earth: Awakening to Your Life's Purpose*[13], Eckhart Tolle believes that thinking without awareness is the fundamental dilemma of human existence. He gives his own example of his awakening shift in consciousness in which his thinking and awareness separated. Instead of being lost in thought, he recognizes himself as the awareness behind it. Can you step back from your thoughts and separate yourself from them? It's as if you distance yourself from your own thoughts and evaluate them objectively. You become the observer.

When you become aware of yourself as the observer, you come to realize that we are a society largely disconnected from our consciousness. It's a scary premise because most of us don't realize we are asleep. Like the move "The Matrix", we're often oblivious that we are in this state. We need to cultivate our awareness consciously in order to be truly present in the moment, allowing us to fully embrace joy and the surrounding beauty, seeing the spirit in everything.

Buddhists call this state "right-mindfulness." Their belief is that we are always giving our attention to something. The attention can be appropriate or inappropriate. When it is appropriate, we are focusing on the present moment. When it is inappropriate, it is taking us away from the here and now. Therefore, mindfulness is coming back into the present moment. Thich Nhat Hanh talks of the seven miracles of mindfulness. We will discuss the first three miracles of mindfulness. The first miracle is to be present and touch deeply the sky, flower, butterfly, friend, spouse, or child. It is not only being present, but it is to touch deeply. Deeply is the operative word. Not only is it important to shift your awareness, it is just as important to give your fullest and deepest attention. It is, "I see you."

The second miracle is to make the sky, flower, butterfly, friend, spouse, or child present as well. This is crucial to mindfulness. Without doing this, you are still asleep. Bringing someone or something into the present requires being awake and fully present. It is almost as if the object of your attention becomes alive. You'll witness a pulsating energy, offering new and unprecedented experiences. Try this exercise: See the flower, sky, or your spouse come alive in spirit. Seeing things like this transforms lives. Experience joy and a new world unfolds. There will be an energy exchange; a vibrational flow.

The third miracle is to nourish what you are giving attention to. This is a true form of love: to "see" the other person — nourish it, love it 100 percent, mind, body, and soul. It's like fusing your soul with the person, place, or thing. Whatever you make your attention, you honor and bless it. You take it into your form. It is in your heart when you give your complete attention. Being with someone or somewhere will always lead to new knowledge. Learn more about a person as you nurture them and witness their growth. Your heart and their heart will open to extra levels that you never thought imaginable.14

When you become a mindful person, you meet someone with your full attention. Have you ever been in a situation where the person you were with kept shifting their gaze and looking elsewhere? Perhaps they were distracted by a phone call or a text? How did that make you feel? If you are busy, you can still give people your full attention, even if it is for a few minutes. It doesn't need to be lengthy, just heartfelt. Meet them as if they were your superhero or role model. Meet them as if you were meeting Jesus or Buddha himself. That is a wonderful exercise when you greet someone. Many nurses use the technique of visualizing their patients as their sister, mother, brother, or other loved one. This allows them to focus and care deeply for the patient. If you think about it, we are all brothers and sisters. From an early age, our society teaches us to care for our immediate family, but rarely for the rest of the community. We encourage you to expand your heart further. One of the most important teachings is to give love and attention to everything you encounter, so you can bring forth joy, compassion, and love. In her book, *Choosing Happiness: Life and Soul Essentials*15, Stephanie Dowrick reminds us to recognize the power we have to influence other people: to lift their spirits, encourage them, listen to them, or show them your care and concern, even for a few moments. What an amazing teaching.

Many of our everyday tasks and routines are performed unconsciously, as we go about our daily lives on autopilot. What about eating? Are you attentive to the food you put in your bodies or do you eat unconsciously, not savoring your meal? Perhaps we feel rushed, so we shovel food into our mouths while we are running to our next encounter. Few people prioritize the simple pleasure of sharing meals as a family. Next time you eat, remember to honor yourself by eating consciously. Fully engage your senses with each bite of food by savoring the taste, identifying the different smells, and appreciating the texture and temperature. You are putting nourishment and the spirit of the animal or plant life in your body. By sitting down to eat, you honor both yourself and the spirit of the plant or animal consumed. Say a simple prayer such as, "May the spirit of the plant and the spirit of the animal bless and nourish our bodies as Creator intended. We say this in a good way." Think about what it takes for even a vegetable to get onto your dinner table. The farmer goes out and cultivates the land, plants the seeds and harvests the vegetable. Next, workers process the food, stack the pallets, and trucks deliver them to the stores. Then, there is another extensive process at the grocery store. Mother Earth had to take on the rain and all the elements so that this plant can grow. You may taste and feel the soil as you eat the plant. You take in its full essence. It's important to be present with the food you eat. To be mindful of the food you are eating. A side benefit is that being mindful helps you eat less, which can be a great weight loss strategy. Europeans spend leisurely meals with multiple courses and breaks for conversation. In contrast, American dining culture tends to value efficiency and speed, with quick service restaurants and on the go eating habits leading to faster meal consumption. Our culture can take a lesson of slowing down and enjoying a slower pace of eating and enjoyment of the food and company.

When we put unhealthy substances in our bodies such as excessive alcohol or other drugs, it is a mind numbing experience. Alcohol and drug addiction can cause individuals to become disengaged or disconnected from experiencing and fully participating in life. It's leads to harmful consequences and disrupt's one's well-being and mental clarity. Addiction may initially serve as a way to numb emotional pain and distress, but ultimately, it leads to destruction. It's a temporary bandaid. Society does not encourage or teach us to confront and sit with our pain. We learn to avoid pain and seek pleasure. It's important to stay present amidst pain and suffering. Without suffering, we cannot grow. Life is not always gooey, yummy gumdrops. So what is the alternative? Do we choose the easy path of substance abuse to avoid pain? Or do we sit in our pain, embrace it, move forward, transcend, and learn from it? Confronting and sitting with our pain is essential for personal growth and healing, as it allows us to process and learn from our experiences rather than avoiding or suppressing them. What is causing you pain? Can you confront and heal it? Sometimes our pain is telling us we need to change, so we need to honor that pain and hear what it has to say. There is no magic pill to make our problems disappear, and following spiritual teachings takes commitment and practice. Select one lesson from this book that resonates with you and commit to applying it in your daily life. Keep a journal to track your progress and stay focused on your growth. If you need help, please seek guidance from a counselor or other professional. We all need help now and then and an objective person can help you see more clearly.

In his book, *The Heart of the Buddha's Teachings*, Thich Nhat Hanh explains the four noble truths that he calls the "cream of the Buddha's teaching." The first is that our suffering is holy if we embrace it and look deeply into it. If we don't, then it is not holy. Second, we need to recognize that we all suffer to some extent in our mind, body, and soul, and we need to recognize the reasons for the cause of our suffering. Third, we need to not cause this suffering, which is to stop all craving. The fourth path is a set of principles that leads to self-awakening and enlightenment. This is called the Noble Eightfold Path: right view, right intention, right speech, right action, right livelihood, right diligence, right mindfulness, and right concentration. Thich Nhat Hanh uses the analogy of being like the earth. With any teaching, just open yourself up to the rain and allow the rain to penetrate the seeds that are buried deep in your consciousness. You only need to open yourself, body, mind, and heart, because the truth is already within you.16 This book is a must read for anyone seeking to learn about basic Buddhist philosophy in a simple and accessible way.

Feeling rushed all the time might be hindering your ability to truly be in the moment. Some people experience FOMO (fear of missing out) and feel compelled to attend every invitation. However, the true reason is complex and contradictory. You may fill your life with anything and everything because you feel you want to create value for your life. Maybe you feel the need to please others or perhaps have anxiety when sitting alone? This running around blocks time for introspection, relaxation, and mindfulness. Self-reflection is important because it helps you align with your life's meaning and purpose. How can you find purpose running around feeling stressed? Are you avoiding slowing down because you are anxious about being alone? Do you feel uncomfortable just being and facing you? Our society has become uncomfortable with just being. Constant busyness often serves as a way to escape from facing our emotions and dealing with them. To effectively deal with our emotions and preserve our mental well-being, it is important to make time for self-reflection and self-care.

Time constraints are an unavoidable aspect of our reality. Timeliness is crucial for employment and other scheduled activities. If you work, you might wake up with the ringing of an alarm. If you don't work, there are still appointments that keep you time focused. The question becomes, how can we be mindful while performing our activities of daily living? What can we do to calm our anxiousness while going from point A to point B? One way to alleviate feelings of anxiety is to not pack your day with too many activities. Perhaps you can schedule a small amount of free time into your daily grind? There is an exercise that many life coaches use called the Wheel of Life. The Wheel of Life is a visual representation of how satisfied or fulfilled you are in various areas of your life. Start by dividing the wheel (like a pie) into different sections. Each section represents a different aspect of your life, such as career, relationships, health, finances, etc. The bigger the slice, the more time you spend in that area. Next, draw a second wheel and divide that one based on what you would actually prefer. So, for example, if you are slicing 1/2 your wheel for work and 1/4 for housework, another 1/4 for taking care of the kids...where is your time? Perhaps in your new wheel you want more time with your spouse or significant other, or time for yourself? The exercise helps you to see each area of your life and assess what's off balance. It's a great tool to identify what areas you want to pay more or less attention to. Google "Wheel of Life" for the exercise and chart. Another awareness exercise is to record how many hours you scroll your phone and internet. Phones can record your hours, so maybe you can commit to lowering your screen time? Encourage your children to spend less time on the phone, TV, and computer, and more time outdoors. No one can deny that technology has brought forth great things in our life. But it's important to remember that life requires a balance of physical, emotional, and spiritual well-being. Does technology outweigh your spirituality? Do we, as a society, relate to our computers and phones more than nature or tending to our spiritual needs? Are we becoming more like our computers, continually processing information and being bombarded by stimuli? Are we slowly forgetting that we are spirits having a human experience? Do we listen to the teachings of the wind or do we listen to google? Can you implement this exercise? For twenty-four hours, do not turn on your computer (except if that is your work) or your TV, and do not use your phone (except for emergencies). Can you do that for one day? Take the challenge. If you have kids, make it a family experiment or contest. Play a board game or just sit around and talk or take a walk in nature. How do you feel when you are without technology? It may feel uncomfortable at first, but that shows you just how addicted you are. Discuss the exercise over dinner.

Society is dedicated to promoting the optimal development and well-being of our children. Our belief is that many planned events will bring them joy, but that's not necessarily the case. Many parents and children feel frazzled as they navigate a day filled with scheduled activities. The pressure to succeed can be exhausting for some children. Maybe you feel the need to be perfect because you were one of those kids? It's important for parents and caregivers to help children prioritize their time and activities in order to prevent them from becoming overwhelmed with busyness. Encouraging balance, downtime, and mindfulness can help children avoid feeling consumed by too many activities. There is nothing wrong with giving kids scheduled activities as long as it's balanced with free time to explore nature or figure out how to entertain themselves. We want our children to be the best, but define "best." Is best a good, moral, happy, and loving person? How about stress free? If you model running around like a chicken with your head cut off, that lesson is what your children will learn despite what you tell them. However, if you slow down and model being stress free, it becomes a powerful teaching tool. When you understand that every step you take is sacred, your children will learn that lesson from you. Your responsibility extends beyond simply chauffeuring them to and from their scheduled activities. It is teaching them to be present.

A Zen story tells of a man on a galloping horse. A bystander yells, "Where are you going?" as the horse and rider gallop past. The horseman replies, "I don't know. Ask the horse." This analogy is like our habit of energy. We constantly run, unable to stop, even when we try to sleep. This includes worrying. Not only have we made our physical bodies a nervous wreck, we've made worry a habit. If you resolve one issue, do you worry about another one? As we've discussed earlier, worrying is like praying for something you don't want. Think about the seriousness of your problem. If you had one year to live, would this particular worry be important? This simple exercise puts your worries into perspective.

Our minds and bodies are so stressed and polluted with inconsequential crap that we make ourselves sick. To be healthy, we must allocate time for healthy habits.

Having a cluttered space can also hinder your ability to focus on the present moment, as it creates unnecessary distractions and mental noise. Clutter is a physical manifestation of your mind being too busy. When our mental and physical spaces become cluttered, it makes it difficult to focus, relax, and maintain a sense of clarity and peace. By decluttering and organizing your space, you can create a sense of calm and clarity in your mind. When we fill our bodies, minds, and homes with junk (such as unhealthy food, negative thoughts, and physical clutter), it can have a negative impact on our souls or inner selves. Our souls are affected by what we consume and surround ourselves with. Prioritizing self-care and mindful living can help you lead a more balanced and fulfilling life.

Indigenous cultures around the world have strong connections to nature and a deep sense of spirituality. Mindfulness practices are commonly incorporated into daily life through rituals, ceremonies, and traditions that promote presence, gratitude, and connection to the natural world. Storytelling, music, dance, and traditional arts are also used as forms of expression and mindfulness. These practices help individuals connect with the natural world, their ancestors, and the spiritual realm. Indigenous cultures offer valuable lessons on mindfulness, spirituality, and environmental stewardship that can benefit individuals and society as a whole.

To summarize, calm the inner chatter of the monkey mind in order to cultivate a state of mindfulness. In today's society, we often find ourselves caught up in busyness in our mind and bodies rather than taking the time to be mindful of our daily habits. If you feel you are going a hundred miles an hour, try to cut that in half. Purposefully walk slower and your heartbeat will follow. Before you step out of bed, commit to a slower pace. When you slow down your body, you can also calm your mind. When you talk, eat, walk, or engage in activities, do it slowly. This will take practice, but soon it will become a habit. When you slow your body and mind, you find peace. When you're at peace, you can practice being mindful. When you become mindful, you discover your sacredness. When you discover your sacredness, you will witness miracles unfolding all around you.

Larry's Aha Moment

Some of my greatest moments are my alone times. My "me" time. I enjoy my company and I am my best friend and I go to great lengths to have quiet time with myself. You are never really alone unless you don't like the person you are with. If you feel bored or angry, it is probably because you don't enjoy your own company. I get some of my spiritual communications early in the morning. That's when I know the spirit communicates with me, directing my teachings, words, actions, and connections. They already help me open up my heart to allow these new things to happen to me, and I get these things just before I get out of bed. It may be for 1/1000 of a second or for a few minutes. God is present at that moment. Often, we become engrossed in teachings, people, and communities, neglecting the true lessons that surround us - the everlasting spirit. We can live in such a tunnel vision, like a horse with blinders, that we forget about the entire universe that is around us. This example I taught in my martial arts class: If a person really wanted to hurt me and all he thought about is to destroy me and bring me down, then it is the way you present yourself to your opponent. How do you choose to stand before that person? Do you stand before them in fear? Do you stand before them with anger, or with jealousy? If you ground yourself to the earth, if you become one with the tree, the sky, everything, why would anyone want to attack you, hurt you, destroy you, or mock you? To attack me is to attack the entire universe.

Being mindful to me is literally taking on all the teachings all around me, including the teachers that show themselves up to me at the right time and really embracing the teachings. The person who calls you on the phone, you might see as an annoyance, but to me it is a blessing because some people's phones never ring, and they are lonely by their choice. Anytime you have a person who calls or visits, they are reaching out for you. Embrace or engage with them, even if just briefly. Hearing your voice might be just what they need. Being mindful is to fully love the person you are with. What do I want people to say about me if I were to die today, living each day like it's my last? The last thing they uttered will stay eternally imprinted on your memory. Ask yourself what is the one thing that you want to leave each person. What kind of impression do you want others to have of you? What do you want them to remember about you? Leave lessons of love and kindness.

Pam's Aha Moment

When I taught sociology for a community college, I had a student that came to me for advice. She felt slighted because her sister had a lot more money and her niece had all these wonderful opportunities to travel overseas, which her daughter did not. She flew here and there, visiting various places, and planning extravagant activities year after year. What I told her was that it isn't about the places she couldn't afford to take her daughter, it is about creating loving memories. My suggestion was for them to have a Friday night picnic in their living room. Actually put down a blanket and have hotdogs and play a board game. I'll bet her daughter will reminisce about Friday nights when she is older. She might say that although she didn't have money growing up, her mom made special time and memories just for the two of them. How could a child not love those memories? It's not about material possessions or traveling extensively throughout Europe and other locations. We buy into the illusion that just sitting still and enjoying a simple, inexpensive family night with our children that we are not giving them enough. Maybe we can teach our children to value the quiet moments of just being together with simple pleasures.

We need to help teach children to be mindful of conflict. When we lived in the National Forest, my son had many friends that stayed with us. There were times when arguments boiled over and they displayed anger. When that happened, I would take the person out under Grandfather tree, smudge them and listen to meditation music. This helped to quiet their mind. I didn't lecture. The teaching was in the silence of the forest. Nature has so many lessons if we quiet our mind and open our hearts to the teachings. Arguments happen — but why yell and scream? How is reacting in that manner helping the situation? If we as adults can't control our reaction, how do we expect our children to? Model the behavior you want to see in your children. Model the behavior that you want to emulate to the world. Be the change that you want to see. If you haven't done this in the past, start now. You got this!

COMMUNICATE IN GRATITUDE, LOVE & KINDNESS

G*ive thanks for unknown blessings already on the way.* - Native American proverb

Gratitude is an important medicine for walking the Red Road. Gratitude is a magical frequency, and it amplifies everything in your life. Gratitude is love's companion. It is so easy to overlook the blessings in our life. Consider that we are alive and possess free will. We often overlook our basic abilities like seeing, walking, talking, and hearing. If you don't understand this, ask a blind, paraplegic, mute, or deaf person. Most of us can wake up and watch a beautiful sunrise and listen to our four-legged and winged brothers and sisters. We have food on our tables, or we can apply for assistance if we don't. We can walk in nature, see the wonders of Mother Earth and breathe in the beautiful scents that encompass her. Mindfully acknowledge gratitude each morning upon waking, focusing on what you have instead of what you lack. Declare love every day. It is an affirmation, giving appreciating to your life, loved ones, and all your blessings. There may be readers facing challenging physical, mental, and spiritual lessons that interfere with navigating your daily life. Although challenging, there are things you can find to be grateful for, even if it is simply being alive. Every day above ground is a good day.

We all have moments of being spoiled and taking things for granted. This chapter reminds us to reflect on our daily blessings. Sometimes we have to nudge our brain to awaken and embrace our blessings. Remember, your subconscious mind is constantly tuning in to the thoughts and words spoken by your conscious mind. If you're expressing negative thoughts at the start of your day, you are programming yourself to have a bad day. Every day, before you get out of bed, before your feet hit the floor, say to yourself or out loud — it's going to be a great day!

Show gratitude to everyone in your life. We sometimes take our loved ones for granted. We forget to tell them how important they are to us. What if you came home to find that your loved one had died? What did you neglect to tell them? Each day is an opportunity to show your loved one's gratitude. It's easy to criticize what they didn't do, but remember to acknowledge their accomplishments. Every morning and every night, declare how important your loved ones are to you. You won't regret it. Tell them how much they mean to you. You can never hear this enough. Life is short, but your loving words and teachings live on forever.

The pursuit of wealth and power often overshadows gratitude in our society. Sometimes, the distractions of the physical world can blind us to the beauty and power of the spiritual realm. It's important to remember that respect should be based on a person's character, values, and actions, rather than just their material possessions or wealth. Often, the emphasis in our upbringing and education is on perceiving through the ego driven mind, rather than connecting with our spiritual center. When we become imprisoned in egoic thought, we forget to thank Creator. Are you old enough to remember the stock market crashing and people were committing suicide because they lost money? People failed to appreciate what they had, they dwelled on their losses instead. Individuals who associate themselves with money, ego, and power are forever unsatisfied because of their unending cravings. We fall into a spin cycle of wanting more, more, and more, and we forget the simple sacred gifts already given to us. When we connect with the higher vibrations of spirit, we learn the valuable lesson of gratitude and acknowledge the abundance of blessings that surround us. We all have reasons to be grateful. Always remember to keep that lesson close to your heart.

Why do certain individuals with very little possess overflowing love and gratitude, while others with great abundance lack a sense of gratitude and happiness? Material possessions are fleeting and external in nature. You can't take it with you. You never see a U-Haul following a hearse. True happiness comes from within, rooted in the depths of one's heart, rather than from external possessions or circumstances. We have much to be grateful for in our country. Appreciate the privilege of reading this book and having the freedom to do so. Other countries are not that fortunate. They could face imprisonment — or worse.

So, how do you put gratitude in your hearts? First, you must consciously want to work at creating positive results in your life. Then you have to understand your power of perception. How you perceive your situation impacts big changes in your life. Once again, reference the above paragraph, where those without money live happily and gratefully. Why is that? Because their perception is that they have abundance. Their mental image of their situation, along with their thoughts, emotions, and beliefs, set themselves up for success. Maybe your present belief pattern is from the past, feeling not enough. Maybe you perceive yourself or your surroundings as limiting or negative? You establish a "poor me" pattern, which creates an ungrateful attitude. This makes you feel separate from other successful people and makes you feel miserable. You might feel you are missing what they have because you are ego measuring. When you are ego measuring yourself, you identify with how much stuff you have and how you appear to others. Your focus lies on external perceptions and evaluations, neglecting your own essence. When you become grateful for what you have and align your knowingness that we are all part of the collective, you realize we are all made of the same stuff — we are all interconnected. When we rewire our thinking toward one of gratitude, we open up to the joy and love in ourselves. We then become a vehicle of love, joy, and gratitude. Try keeping a gratitude journal, perform acts of kindness, or volunteer for those less fortunate. These small steps help cultivate gratitude.

How do you interact with your relations? Do you communicate lovingly? Is every encounter a heartfelt one? One of the central tenants of the Red Road, and gathering our spiritual medicines, is the loving communication between souls. Actual communication is a spiritual heart felt connection you make that goes beyond verbal and nonverbal communication. When you talk to any person you meet, connect fully and deeply with them. Touch the person's soul. You can achieve this when your soul is vibrating loving energy and joy flows from your heart. It is as if a light of love projects from your heart into the other person's form. It is a form of unspoken communication that often goes unnoticed or unacknowledged. If you think about it, isn't that how Jesus communicated? This form of communication is common among all great spiritual teachers. They all projected loving communication from their hearts. Have you experienced the love of a great teacher in person? Incredible healings occur through this form of communication. Jesus healed others because his love emitted such a powerful vibration. Love and gratitude communicate healing energy, bringing a sense of peace to your mind, body, and soul. You can harness this and be a powerful instrument of healing energy that you are meant to be.

We don't realize how much we can impact others by lovingly communicating. We were made to project every gesture, word, or thought with loving energy. Imagine if we touched every person's heart that we met. What impact can you foresee? How might this alter the world? Imagine the healing that would take place. Everywhere you go, every person you meet, you are communicating not just with words, but with your spiritual energy. Imagine if we could be like a lighthouse projecting our light. We would experience ultimate joy and healing! Try it for a day, a week, a month. It will soon become part of your form. Commit that every person you meet, you are going to interact lovingly. We must practice these techniques; otherwise, they're just words on a page. It's easy to agree, but we need to focus our intent on gratitude and put it into our form.

The world is filled with an endless array of vibrational energies that surround us at all times, shaping our experiences and interactions with the environment. It is important that our vibrational energy support gratitude and loving kindness. Reflect on your most recent visit to a crowded and anxious place. Could you feel the room's energy? What you are feeling is the collective energy of the group. It is a form of vibrational energy that can make you feel comfortable or uncomfortable. If you had the urge to leave the room without knowing the reason, you might be sensitive to this unseen form of communication. There is an innate vibrational energy that we emit, even if we are not aware that we are projecting it. Our senses pick up energy. Try it. When at a gathering, practice sensing the energy. Our bodies emit unseen energy fields known as auras, which vibrate and interact with the energies of the people around us. Embracing the concept of auras can offer a new perspective on our experiences and interactions, enabling us to cultivate a greater sense of balance and harmony within ourselves and the world.

Verbal communication is another form of vibrational energy. We can use the same words, but depending on our tone, pitch, and inflection, there can be different meanings. Your words have power. They can heal, and they can hurt. When you are gathering your spiritual medicines, you know your words need to be kind, honest, and true. Prior to speaking or acting, consider if your words or actions are kind. If not, refrain from speaking. Sometimes we communicate things that are kind but are not true. Your words should always speak the truth. Remember this one important truth; you are spirit having a human experience. If you wake up in the morning and remember that one fact, you are remembering an important original instruction. Our society is reactive and we speak out hastily, but when stressed, breathe deeply, count to 10, and pause before responding. We've all been in a position where we react and later feel remorse, but know this is not walking the Good Red Road.

Nonverbal communication is also a powerful vibration. It involves the use of body language, facial expressions, gestures, tone of voice, and other nonverbal cues to convey messages and emotions. It is your body's response to what you are thinking and feeling. Have you ever been around a person who is verbally saying one thing but their body language tells another story? Try to cue into the body language of the person as they are speaking and be cognizant of your body language. Is your body language positive? Do you walk straight, shoulders back, and smile? Consider your nonverbal communication with the world. What message do you think a frown or being hunched over sends? How does it make you and others feel? When you walk with a confident stride and smile, it can automatically brighten your disposition. Other people around you will respond favorably. If you change small behaviors, you can change how you feel and how people respond to you. By paying attention to the energy we project through our nonverbal communication, we can better understand the impact we have on others and cultivate more meaningful and authentic interactions.

When we communicate, know that issues arise when we try to read other people's minds or expect other people to read our minds. We may get upset because we feel our loved ones should have known better or we think the neighbor is mad at us because they didn't respond to us the way we thought they should have. Then we fabricate our own story of why it happened and soon we find ourselves caught up in our emotions. We often exaggerate small things that frequently are simple misunderstandings, or the person had no clue. That's how drama is created.

One reason marriages collapse is because of poor communication. Women guys can't read your minds. Men, women can't read your minds. Ask for what you want. Use your words. What is obvious to you might not be obvious to your spouse. If something is missing in your relationship, talk kindly about it. It's similar to a hole in a sweater. If you don't mend it, the hole will get bigger and bigger. Don't live in fear of how the other person might respond. Fear is the opposite of love. Many people in relationships have difficulty speaking the truth because they are afraid their loved one might leave them or respond in undue anger. If it's true, what does it say about your relationship? If you are fearful in your relationship, is that coming from you or your spouse? Do you want to keep peace so badly that you can't speak your truth? Or worse, is your spouse going to physically or emotionally hurt you? If your spouse will not hurt you, then why wouldn't you speak your truth? Does this stem from a blockage in your childhood? If you want more attention, ask for it. More importantly, when you catch your spouse doing something you like, tell them. Wouldn't you feel inclined to repeat the same behavior if someone commented on how wonderful it made you feel? The reality is no marriage or relationship is perfect. No one is perfect, but poor communication can certainly break even the best of marriages. Other couples may lack common interests, but still share love, respect, and communication. When you communicate, do so with an open and loving heart. If you have trouble in your marriage communicating, there are marriage counselors to help you navigate issues.

Listen with your ears, your eyes, and your heart. Learn from the voices of the earth and the wisdom of the elders.
 — Native American Proverb

Listening is such an important aspect of communication. Many talk, few listen. Sometimes we need to talk and process our issues or troubles, but there are times we need to listen. Our greatest gift we can give others is to listen with love and gratitude. This is a difficult teaching, because our immediate reaction is to give advice. However, most people do not want advice; they just want to process what is in their head. Once they say it out loud, they may come up with their own solutions. Men often like to fix problems, while women may simply need a sympathetic ear. Listen and observe the other person's nonverbal cues. Work on resisting the urge to think of a response in your head. When we think about how we are going to respond, we lose most of the conversation. Focus intently on what the person is saying, verbally and nonverbally. Avoid distractions and give your full, undivided attention. People want to be heard with your mind, body, and soul. They need to feel special, and listening equates to caring. You don't have to listen for hours; just give that person ample time. When you truly love your brother or sister, give them the precious gift of listening from your heart.

It is difficult to find the time to listen in this busy world, and we sometimes rank in our head who is and who is not, listen-worthy. We might not make time to listen to our elders or our children. However, there are great lessons to be learned by listening to the forgotten ones. We might want people to get to the point, but we miss so much when we have this attitude. Elders and children may not always communicate in the way we expect, but they offer us valuable teachings and wisdom. The Native Americans revered their elders and honored their teachings. They are the Wisdom Keepers and play a vital role in preserving and sharing the cultural heritage and wisdom of their communities. Many other cultures revere their elders as well. Our society often places high value on the wisdom of those with power and wealth, but this can be seen as an illusion. There are teachings in the wind, sky, rainbow, and many hidden lessons in plant and animal forms. Open up your mind, body, and soul; listen to their voices.

Communication also takes place with the spirit world and the plants, animals, and rocks. There is a big communication gap on the part of the two-legged. We consider ourselves superior, and some people don't even realize everything communicates. The spirit world, plants, animals, and rocks are always available to support and assist us. Some people scoff at the absurdity of this premise. But as we discussed in a previous chapter, the animal and plant life can be our greatest teachers. How can we be so arrogant to think we are the only ones that know how to communicate? Look at the medicines that the animal and plant life give us. Look at what they offer for us when they provide us with sustenance. Mother Earth provides so much for us, and we don't even listen to her when she cries out for help. Like everything else, her cries fall to deaf ears. Our hearts have been desensitized to the destruction we bring to everything we touch. We are like parasites sucking the living life out of everything without replenishing. Thank God there are programs, organizations, and people that are bringing awareness to the balance of nature and our future. We hope this trend continues, so balance can be restored.

There is a thin veil that separates us from the spirit world. We can open up our communication to the spirit world to receive messages from our loved ones who have crossed over. Rainbows, animals, whispers, songs, dreams, scents, or other forms of communication can convey messages from your loved ones. Open a channel to their presence by opening your heart and call to them. This is a natural process if we are willing to open communication with the spirit world. We can train ourselves by asking, praying, honoring, listening, and raising our vibration. Take the time and open your heart to their messages.

When we have communication conflicts, people sometimes yell, argue, abuse, or hurt others. There are domestic violence problems in our society. If this is happening to you, we urge you to call local authorities or domestic violence hotlines. There is support, resources, and assistance to individuals experiencing domestic violence. This is something that should not be happening in any culture. Unfortunately, drugs, alcohol and stress are a big reason this is happening in today's world. Many individuals are reconnecting with traditional Red Road teachings as a means of addressing their struggles with alcohol and drug addiction. By adhering to Red Road teachings, we understand the importance of abstaining from alcohol and drugs. There are many therapeutic programs that can help, and we encourage anyone having issues to please honor yourself by reaching out for help. As spiritual beings, remember to seek guidance from Creator and acknowledge your unique abilities and contributions. We all have valuable gifts to bring to the table. Native American culture was tied to their belief system and their love for their land and people. Healing of a tribe member involved community, medicine, and spiritual healers. It was a holistic approach, and no one was looked down upon. All the people were taken care of; even the two-spirited people were highly regarded. Look at what we do to people who are ill in our culture. Mental imbalance is still a stigma in this society. It is the silent suffering that individuals face that leads to feelings of inadequacy and failure. We need to do better. What if we ensured that every person's needs were met and their well-being was a top priority? People can claim they are Christian or spiritual, but if they harm each other in any way, this proves otherwise. Imagine if we all communicated in a kind and loving way? Let's make a conscious choice to be spiritual conduits!

To summarize, communicate in loving and grateful ways. Think about the small gestures you can do on a daily basis to touch people's lives. Just three words, "I love you," hold immense power. Loving and kind communication is one of the most important jobs we have. Everything you touch in loving communication can be your gift to others. It is this knowing that can bring joy and peace to your heart. Please don't minimize your power to influence your life and those around you with loving communication. What if we communicated to someone how they touched our life? Can you just imagine the joy you would bring to that person? Don't wait until someone dies and then speak at their funeral. Tell them now. If you leave this world tomorrow, how would you want people to remember you? Your words and teachings will never be forgotten. Their vibrational energy reverberates indefinitely, leaving a lasting imprint on the world.

Larry's aha moment

I've received countless wonderful gifts that left me in awe. I am grateful for the journey that made me who I am today, both the positives and negatives. I'm grateful for teachers who entered my life, even those who became enemies, as they bring back teachings. Some of my best teachings came from hard life lessons.

I'm grateful for being a dad, being there for my children throughout their lives. They changed my life completely, along with my loving wife. I love her deeply and completely. I've known her since the eighth grade, and she has been my soul mate, my rock, and she has been behind me 110 percent, and half the time I didn't know she was behind me. She has supported me in her own little hidden ways, and she is the most wonderful person in my whole life. We have been married for almost 50 years. What a wonderful and beautiful lady, and I hope we stay together forever.

Native Americans often get their communication and teachings from the sweat lodge, from the rocks and water. In ancient times, the world was formed with spirit. But an elder once told me when plant life was first created in the world, there was in abundance and beauty. So Creator put forth the four-legged and the two-legged and the ones that fly and crawl. When he created man, man began killing many animals. The animals were being harvested at a rapid rate to sustain and comfort man. There's a story that all the animal life came together in council and they decided that for all the different animals man would kill, they would create a disease to befoul and harm man. Yet, the plants were friends to humans, and they also had council. The plants decided that for every disease that the animals created, they were going to lend their bark, their roots, and their leaves to cure man. That is how the laws of the universe ended up working hand in hand—instead of one killing one another, one started helping. Certain individuals communicate by openly conversing with and visiting animals, resulting in profound teachings. And though some people are so connected to Mother Earth, they know when she is hurting. They have that personal connection. They can sense the state of a particular plant, animal, or spirit life and communicate with them, receiving their particular teachings—and they have so many lessons. When we do a prayer over our meal, we are praying for the plant or animal for their nourishment, so it lives on through us or as spirit to continue their growth. There might be certain sounds that present themselves to you with no form. They are the spirit of life that is around you. It is making it known to you that they are speaking in this language. Open-hearted and open-soul individuals understand this. This is the communication of the silent world. Dreams can also communicate from the spirit world. Open yourself to day and night messages. Listen to your dreams to understand your unconscious messages. Why not interpret your nighttime messages? It can lead you on a new journey.

One of the most powerful forms of communication I received was when I met the Dalai Lama. When he and I actually made contact, he held his hands together as though he was praying, and he pointed his two hands as they were together right to me, and he said in a whispering voice, "Find the lesson in everything that happens to you." I've always kept that lesson deep within my soul.

I've also had some amazing martial arts teachers that taught me many lessons, including ways to keep calm in violent moments so I could perform. Some of my greatest teachings were from my many years of martial arts training. It takes a disciplined form of communication from your body, mind, and soul to perform martial arts.

Some of my teachings come in simple forms of communication as well. I remember when I was at a festival watching a child in his dad's arms who squirmed to get down. When he did, he ran toward a piece of trash and picked it up and threw it in the garbage. This inspired others to pick up trash, creating a chain of events. The next thing I knew, everyone seemed to be picking up trash. It was a beautiful scene. An act of one child started this event. I seem to come across one every day or I reveal to one every day. These things magically appear to you when you walk in spirit.

Pamela's aha moment

I think there are times in our lives when we forget to be grateful. When I committed to bring forth spiritual lessons of being grateful on a daily basis, joy unfolded. Being happy is putting gratitude in your form. I believe that 100 percent! I am especially grateful for my husband David, who supports my authentic self. This book would only be in my head and not published, if not for his encouragement to write down my spiritual teachings. I realize my soul's purpose is to communicate and encourage people to live their best authentic life, knowing true spiritual oneness. We are all in this together...evolving and learning on this planet. I know it's difficult to be grateful when crap hits the fan... we've all been there...but gratitude during those times slowly leads you out of darkness into the light.

My dreams have opened up a whole new world for me. I've had many ceremonial dreams with my spirit guide, Clap Dance, and I'm so grateful to him. He led me to my husband, my hospice career, and also many spiritual awakenings. I am grateful for every dream and vision. I've trusted and listened to my dreams and when instructed, I would give messages. I remember one particular dream where I was instructed to give my boss a message. The message was difficult as I had just started the job and didn't know her well. Three of her spirit guides came to my spirit guide, and they were not happy. They stomped their feet because she wasn't listening to them. They asked my guide if it was okay to give me the message. The message was quite serious in nature. Her husband was depressed, her daughter suicidal, and they wanted her to quit her job. My boss had a serious demeanor, so I had no way of knowing how she would respond. I relayed the message and remember her asking me to repeat what I said. She didn't say much, but a couple of days later she quit her job and I never heard from her again.

I had a good friend who committed suicide. He was in trouble financially and was worried about providing for his disabled wife. What he didn't realize was that money did not matter to her. He didn't realize he was more than just a financial statement, he could not let go of that aspect of his life. He was one of the most loving, passionate, compassionate, talented, and kindest man I've had the pleasure of knowing. He had friends, family, and a spouse who loved him. He lost sight of that fact, and now he is gone. Please don't lose sight. Communicate if you are feeling depressed or suicidal. There is help out there. 988 is the suicide hotline. This is an extreme example, but when we lose a touch of gratitude and communication, we slowly lose a part of ourselves.

Larry Running Turtle and Pamela Two Spirits

When we talk about using kind and loving communication and being grateful on the Red Road, this includes you as well. Don't be hard on yourself. Remember that earth is one big school and we are all in this together. No one is perfect and we all have different life lessons. Choose to communicate with yourself in a positive, kind, and loving way.

CRABS IN THE BARREL SYNDROME

L *ove one another and do not strive for another's undoing.* — Seneca

Crabs in the barrel occurs when a like-minded group prevents advancement within their community. They refuse to work together and distrust the rest of the group. The philosophy is, "If I can't have it, neither can you." There are some people who are not connected to spirit and feel they are stuck in their life's position. They don't want to see anyone succeed, so they bring them down with criticism, negativity, and/or gossip.

When crabs are caught and placed in a container, they pinch each other instead of trying to escape. There are these unhappy, status quo crabs in a barrel. They're all hanging out, complaining, with no one breaking free. Occasionally, a crab has had enough and decides he wants to change his situation. Negativity is not getting him anywhere, and he decides he wants to succeed. He struggles and struggles, climbing on top of all the crabs, and he finally reaches the top of the barrel. Crabs being crabs, the others always pull that one crab down. He has no chance to succeed. The crabs hold him captive.

Can you think of any group of people that you have been around, either at work or in your personal life, that always seem to complain, not taking initiative or responsibility for their life? It seems like some people don't want to change their situation and don't want anyone else changing theirs either. People will sit, complain, criticize, and declare what's wrong with others. They point fingers and blame everyone else. If a crab dislikes its surroundings and tries to escape, the others don't support it. They don't want that person deviating from their norm of negativity and being stuck. They want everyone to be unhappy. You know the old saying; misery loves company. They don't understand that life's progression is a choice and it can be more than just winners and losers.

Sometimes the emotion driving the group is fear. Fear of others excelling or one of them falling behind the group. In a Caribbean newspaper, the tagline "crabs in a barrel" caught our attention. An owner of a commercial waterfront building rented space to many tourist trinket booths. He decided he wanted to raise the rent of the booths. He was also willing to just sell the building outright for a fair price. The vendors formed an organization to negotiate the new lease and possibly fund buying the building instead of renting. They argued with each other and some refused to cooperate. The holdouts feared some would get more benefits. Consequently, the entire group had to pay increased rent and forego ownership of a commercial building. The native islanders had the chance to move from selling trinkets to owning the property outright but couldn't bring themselves to cooperate.

You may be working towards self-improvement or career advancement, only to face unexpected obstacles or sabotage. They draw you back down to their level to prevent you from reaching higher levels of yourself. Maybe they gossip about you or make fun of you about your recent choices you are making. They have become the crabs in the barrel. Just as you're about to succeed, they choose to drag you down instead of helping you. It's easy to feel discouraged and believe you can't break free. Do not succumb to their negativity and start believing that you can't get ahead. You may even feel defeated and help pull other crabs down. You took the bate; hook, line and sinker.

Just being aware of the "crabs in the barrel" syndrome can help you persevere. You know in your heart that sitting around complaining or not taking initiative is unproductive. Take charge of your life, no matter what anyone throws at you. If you have good intent, why bring other people's criticism into your being? If you sit and do nothing, what have you accomplished? How is that going to change anything? We all have some fear of making mistakes, but why let it hinder your growth? Follow your heart instead of your fear. The first door you enter may not be perfect, but it leads to other doors.

Don't get caught up in negative energy and drama. Run! Do you want to associate with negative people who are always complaining about other people? Or would you rather be around those who promote, encourage, and love you? Are you allowing negative people to impact your life? More importantly, are you promoting, encouraging, and loving yourself despite what others say?

We all know jealous, negative, or just plain critical people. The most important lesson they teach is to not take things personally. It's not about you, but about who they are. Take responsibility for your own life and don't worry about the people who are trying to bring you down. Stay in your own lane. Losing focus and doubting oneself means living others' desired life, not your own. Honor yourself by realizing there is no greater teacher than the one you already have — you.

Now let's talk. What if you are the problem of your situation? If so, take responsibility to change it. We all have times in our lives when we realized our attitudes could have helped or hindered a situation. It's important to recognize that you can change your story. Soar, like the eagle we know you can be! There is an analogy involving an eagle and a duck. We can choose to bring forth an eagle spirit or a duck spirit. In any situation, you will see a few-eagle spirited people and, unfortunately, a lot of duck people. What that translates to is that there are people we know who do duck things; they are whiners, complainers, users, they just quack, quack, quack, following each other around, complaining about many things. They tell you how things are not working in the world vs things that are. When you bring up solutions to a problem, they will tell you 100 reasons it won't work.

Eagle people have the natural skills to do any job well. In a work situation, if you hire people who are friendly and outgoing, you don't have to train them to smile. They are eagle people. If you go into an establishment and ask for service and they let you know they don't feel like doing anything for you, that is a duck. An eagle person will make things happen with no recognition. They will just take care of it themselves and go above and beyond expectations. They will soar above and treat you like they want to be treated. Ask yourself in any situation if you are being a duck or an eagle.

In summary, there are people in this world that complain and will try to bring you down to their level. Don't take the bait. Don't react — be the person who does something about a situation. Complaining solves nada. As intuitive, spiritual beings, you know to follow your heart. If you stay true to this spiritual medicine, the negative people in your life will not influence you. You will be strong and grounded like Grandfather tree. Be flexible, but remain grounded in Mother Earth when negative people enter your life.

Larry's Aha Moment

For 150 years, there wasn't a Native American Coming of Age ceremony performed in the State of Texas. Remember, it was not legal for Native Americans to conduct ceremonies in the state until the American Indian Religious Freedom Act (AIRFA) was signed in 1978. Several years ago, Elder Domingo Carillio revived the ceremony in Southeast Texas. The Coming of Age is when a young lady is coming up to young womanhood in Native American culture. This ceremony existed in the Native American culture prior to Europeans arrived, and the invading Spaniards had a similar ceremony. The modern Mexican quinceañera actually has Aztec and Spanish roots.

The Coming of Age ceremony is a vigorous ceremony, taking three or four days to complete. Sometimes it is only two days, but the ceremony always entails elder women coming around the young women coming of age that year and coaching, molding, and shaping them into the woman they are about to become. The women invite a local Wisdom Keeper to come in and conduct the ceremonies. We conduct ceremonies as taught and counsel young ladies through their transition to womanhood.

Around 20 years ago, I received an invitation as the Wisdom Keeper to conduct the inaugural Coming of Age ceremony, which lasted three days. It is a time of little sleep and constant prayers done inside the tepee for these young ladies. They hadn't conducted this ceremony in over a hundred and fifty years. I caught a lot of flak for conducting it because not only did we make history, but also our own Native American people saw it as a threat, and some did everything to bring me down. Some asked why I was the Wisdom Keeper invited and what right did I have to conduct that ceremony. Instead of helping me and guiding me, these crabs tried to bring me down. On the flip side, other Native Americans praised and honored me for the ceremony. We've conducted the ceremony annually since then and, fortunately, pushed these naysayers aside. We continue to do the ceremonies year after year.

One of my early spiritual lessons from one of my teachers was to always surround myself with positive people. Once that seed was planted, I made an effort to surround myself with spiritual masters and positive, uplifting people. The more I looked for them, the more they appeared in my life. In my youth, I was seen as odd for spending time with older individuals. I was like a sponge, always absorbing teachings. My neighborhood had a lot of negativity, drugs, drinking, fights, gangs, and once in a while I hung out with them. People labeled me, but I was not involved with negative activity. I surrounded myself with excellent role models, and I still do to this day. I've always sought spirituality, wanting to learn more about it. The more I learned, the less I knew. There is so much information and a lot of teachers out there and not enough time to consume it all.

Pam's Aha moment

I remember an incidence when a co-worker was dissuading a young college student from becoming a nurse. The student was so excited and nursing called to her heart. My co-worker was a nurse herself and was dissatisfied with her position. She shared all the profession's negatives with the student. When the student came to me for advice, I gave her encouragement and truth. Nurses have endless possibilities and opportunities. In labor and delivery, you welcome life; in hospice, you transition life. You can educate other potential nurses, work in an office, work independently, at home health, etc... I told her the choices were endless and you would never have to feel stuck unless you chose to be. Lastly, I said follow your heart because it will help you in your decisions.

I've had employees try to sabotage me at work, but what I've learned was to stay in my lane. People can be jealous because you are happy doing your job. I refused to put energy into their negative attitudes and promised myself that I will not change my positive being into their negative one. They wanted me frustrated and angry, so I'd join them at the bottom. I was called a Pollyanna many times at my jobs and I learned to laugh at that and agree!

FORGIVING AND LETTING GO

T*he weak can never forgive. Forgiveness is the attribute of the strong.*
— Mohandas Gandhi

We must develop and maintain the capacity to forgive. He who is devoid of the power to forgive is devoid of the power to love
— Martin Luther King, Jr

In our lives, everyone has experienced some sort of trauma, drama, or karma. We all have some sort of baggage that we carry around with us. How can we move forward carrying all that baggage? How can we release the pain to progress? Trauma comes in many forms, and as individuals, we respond to it differently. You could have experienced trauma in your childhood from emotional, physical, or other abuses. You may have had a joyful childhood, yet adulthood brought the hardships of divorce, death, or financial struggles. Stressful events touch all of us. Can you remember your last major stressor? How did it impact your life? Some people quickly release past hurts. For others, it takes more time. However, there are some people who continue to relive the encounter repeatedly, continuing to carry their baggage with them year after year. This chapter talks about how to release your baggage for a healthier, happier life.

Loss has to be processed physically, emotionally, and spiritually, but it doesn't have to continue to hurt us throughout our lives once we've processed it. Buddha compared remembering a wrong to a burden on the mind. He says that holding on to anger is like grasping a hot coal with the intent of throwing it at someone else, but you are the one who gets burned. Haven't you heard people say, "I remember in high school when they made fun of me..." and they recount it like it was yesterday and they still cling to the hurt and anger it caused them? It might have been fifty years ago, but they are still carrying it around. What good does that do? At a certain point in life, you close one chapter and begin another. Not that you forget it ever happened, you just decide to stop constantly reliving every detail. You stop allowing the hurt and anger to continue.

One of the best ways to stop past events from continuing to hurt is by learning to forgive. Forgiveness enables us to release the past and embrace the present. It brings peace that allows you to focus on yourself and helps you get on with life. When we realize and understand that we are all interconnected, we understand our human form is not perfect. We all make mistakes, whether or not the mistakes are intentional. We have hurt others and others have hurt us. Learn to step away from your human emotion and embrace the compassion and love you have in your heart. You can say that your human self does not understand the particular situation or action, but your spiritual self knows that we are all here to learn lessons and evolve. Look at the situation from spirit's perspective. Embrace forgiveness because without it, over time, we become hardened with anger. Who wants to go about life angry? If you dissect or peel away anger, you will find hurt. When you forgive, you heal your hurt and the anger slowly dissipates. You then feel lighter and freer, and more importantly, it allows you to move forward and live a happier life. You have the choice whether to be friends with the people that hurt you. Maybe in time you will, but your primary responsibility is to forgive... for you — to heal yourself. Forgiveness takes time and reflection, so be patient with yourself. If only we could forgive as fast as our furry friends. It's so easy for them to forgive; maybe that is why we love animals so much. All they ask is that we be present with them. What a gift they are!

Stephanie Dowrick, in *Choosing Happiness17*, talks about forgiveness as the most demanding of all the qualities. In today's society, it is also the most essential. Our world is dominated by revenge cycles and bitterness in countless encounters, from private to public. Reflect on our planet's history. We humans have done atrocious things to masses of our fellow humans. We have caused much, much pain in many situations. Forgiving and learning from our past is crucial for the human race. If we don't learn from the past, how can we learn from our mistakes? How can we move forward as a society and transcend into a loving, accepting, and a non-judging one? We have to start with ourselves as mirrors so the world can reflect upon us. We easily complain that the world is so unforgiving and does atrocious things, but we can't even forgive our friend, family, or neighbor. It starts there.

A centuries old native Hawaiian forgiveness ritual called *Ho'oponopono18* embraces oneness through forgiveness. You can implement this technique for any problem. It can be used face to face, on the phone, or even if the person is absent. It's also therapeutic when you need to heal a relationship when that person has passed away. Use Ho'oponopono if you have a judgmental thought about a friend or a random person. The core belief of this ritual is that we can heal ourselves and the world if we can become free of everything that is not love. Ho'oponopono removes all negative effects on our memories and cleanses us, so we can once again become a reflection of light and love. To accomplish this, Ho'oponopono relies on 4 sentences: I am sorry, please forgive me, I love you, and thank you. What do these four sentences mean?

I am sorry.

I apologize. I have perceived suffering (in myself or others) and I am sorry for that. I no longer reject the problem, but recognize the role my consciousness has played in mine or another's suffering. I understand that anything that comes to my awareness couldn't be there unless it wasn't already within me (my consciousness). I know where I stand and feel remorse.

Please forgive me.

Forgive me for consciously or unconsciously having created chaos and disturbance for you and me. Please forgive me for having acted contrary to the divine laws of harmony and love. Please forgive me for having until now judged you (or the situation), and in the past disregarded our spiritual identity and connectedness. I now hold no judgement and recognize we are all part of each other.

I love you.

I love you and I love myself. I see and respect the divine in you. I love and accept the situation just as it is. I love you and myself with all our weaknesses and faults. I reaffirm that every situation that has shown up as a problem brings me back to my true, divine nature.

Thank you.

Thank you, for I understand the miracle is already underway. I thank God and the angels for transforming my request. I give thanks, because through the power of forgiveness, I am freed from the energetic chains of the past. I give thanks I may recognize and join with the Source of all Being.

Whenever you have an issue with something or someone in your life, repeat the 4 sentences. This cleanses you and makes room for divine love to pour into you. Ho'oponopono helps heal the person asking forgiveness and all the people involved. Google Dr. Hew Len, a clinical psychologist, healed a ward of mentally ill criminals using Ho'oponopono. It's a fascinating read. There are many counselors and hypnotherapists that use this technique knowing that it is a profound framework for healing, growth, and self-discovery.

Do you find it hard to forgive yourself? Why is that? Does this stem from childhood or a past relationship? Do you expect to be perfect? Do you forget that life is one big lesson? We all evolve, and we all have made mistakes we are not proud of. When we can't forgive ourselves, how can we forgive others? Our self-criticism spills over into our judgement of others. If we expect to be perfect, we look for perfection in others as well. We all make mistakes. If you don't learn and move on, did you learn? We are imperfect, just like the world. As Mother Theresa points out in the book *A Gift for God*, "I would rather make mistakes in kindness and compassion than work miracles in unkindness and hardness." 19 We will talk more about perfection in a later chapter.

Releasing the need to be right is necessary for forgiveness. Is our goal to be proven right, or is it to experience true happiness? Releasing control and ego is crucial. Letting go allows us to see the bigger picture. We have to be the bigger person and understand that despite someone's actions, we just need to move forward. We all have friends who can be excessively nosey, overly talkative, opinionated, or brutally honest — the list is endless. What you have to ask yourself is what was the intent behind the person's actions? We all come from different life experiences and perceptions. When certain people come into your path, they come to give you lessons of what you have forgotten on your spiritual path. Viewing them this way removes negativity. Christ, even when spit upon, saw their souls, not their projections. He took everyone into his heart, even the sinners, the prostitute and the tax man. The biggest act of love we can give to others is to forgive them.

Forgiveness becomes more difficult when there was bad intent. In those circumstances, we have to reach deep within our souls to make peace with the situation. Is this person intentionally continuing to hurt you? In that case, reconsider the relationship. Boundaries are important, and if someone continues to disregard your boundaries, sometimes you need to let the relationship go with forgiveness in a peaceful, respectful way. You need to honor yourself first and foremost.

If the person has good intent most of the time but has occasional flub ups, then maybe you can open your heart and understand that when we act bad, we are coming from our disobedient inner child. We are not acting like adults. And when the person who hurts us acts like a child and we don't forgive, we are coming from our inner child as well. We say, "Fine, you hurt me, so I hurt you." So there.

How do you heal a loss such as divorce or grief? If we are old enough, we have all experienced pain and grief. Grieving is a natural process that follows any loss. Time and a counselor can aid you in this challenging phase. After a period, we learn to let our pain process through our loss. We learn to grow spiritually from the situation. Everyone experiences hurt and anger, but if we continue to carry it around, we will inhibit our spiritual and emotional growth. We get stuck reliving the experience, and slowly we become bitter and depressed. When we forgive the pain of divorce, loss, or grief; we move forward with our lives, knowing there is purpose.

With death, we can let go by releasing balloons, scattering ashes, writing a letter, or other ceremonies to help release the pain in our hearts. It is painful when our loved ones die, but we choose life because we know that we, too, will die someday. We live in faith that we will all be together soon enough. We are spirits having a human experience. What about divorce? Ceremonies are possible for divorce as well. There are divorce ceremonies that are meant to help people move forward. Try to accept the lesson and move on. If this is difficult to do, write a letter and burn it or have a personal ceremony.

To summarize, forgiveness and letting go is an essential spiritual practice to help you move forward to live your best life possible. When we continue to hold on to our anger and hurt, it holds us back. Forgive yourself and others to live your best life possible. Pray to Creator to help you in the forgiveness process. It may take time, but it will happen. Letting go is not a simple process, but it is important. When we let go, our vessel is free to fill up with love.

Larry's Aha Moment

I conduct many ceremonies back home, and one of these ceremonies is a "spirit release" ceremony. When a certain loved one passes away, we do a "spirit release" ceremony. People ask me to perform, but on the scheduled day, they refuse to let go and cancel the ceremony. There are countless other ones where we did release the spirit of their loved ones and then they went on with their lives as I did with my parents. We hold the belief that spirits remain for a year, bound by unfinished tasks. After that, we burn sage, offer tobacco, light the pipe, and release them. And how we know the spirit was accepted is by seeing a falling star. The spirit's acceptance by the star people confirms the soul's return to earth.

We perform straightforward rituals for animals and the deceased, using corn or tobacco, in order to preserve their spirits. We do ceremonies for those who are so attached to this animal. They can ease their pain a little, knowing that there is comfort in spirit and ceremony and that the animal has made it to its rightful place.

Watching my mother depart and join the spirit realm was a painful experience for us. We were in the hospital saying our ishkas (which means "until I see you again") to Mom while we were gathered around in a circle praying over her. I remember seeing the heart monitor, and when it flatlined, it was like an arrow shot through my heart. I never knew what a broken heart felt like until that moment. As Native people, we have giveaways after a loved one dies, so we brought all my mom's belongings together, and everyone gets a certain number. And if you picked that certain number, you get that particular pile of stuff. There were six siblings, and as the numbers were being read off, each one had a particular pile we would pick from. One sibling was getting mad at another one because one of them owned something they wanted to own. They were not letting go of it and did not understand its ceremonial aspect. I recall entering the house during that time, hearing my siblings yelling and cursing in frustration over those specific items. I closed the door, and my father was waiting outside, and I told him that there was nothing in that room that I could want that would bring Mom back. They could fight for it, but I didn't want a part of it. All I cared about was that Mom was here in my heart and no one could take that away from me. And my dad was happy to hear that, and he had already set aside what he wanted to give me, which was her medicine bag that she always carried and a few blankets that were given to her as a gift during her naming ceremony and other ceremonies.

Almost for a month, I struggled with my mother's death. I cut off all my hair and became distant towards everyone. I remember having my coffee in my mother's backyard when my father came out and saw me crying. He put a hand on my shoulder and said, "Son, you need to let her rest." What he told me next was something that I never expected from him because my stepfather was not Indian; he was Hispanic, although he embraced the Native culture. He suggested I embrace the wind as my mother. Thus, when I emerge to greet the holy ones, I will feel my mother's gentle touch first. And he reminded me that she will embrace me day by day and will remind me to comb my hair, to stand up straight, and to be stronger. This was one of the greatest teachings I could have had. No longer did I mourn her. It was like a faucet being turned off. Four years later, my father died from smoking. The next day was my birthday, and I did a ceremony, and I adopted the sun to be my father because I remembered his teachings. This way, when I wake up each morning, I get to greet my mother and father. He is with me all day long, along with my mother. Many of us, like myself, share teachings and upbringing with our ancestors, which is why we feel spiritually connected to Mother Earth. We've adopted trees, clouds, and water, and when we see the water and the sky being polluted and the trees clear-cut, may they realize that these are our people — these are our relations.

Pam's Aha Moment

At a young age, I learned the importance of forgiving and letting go. It was difficult, and at times, I needed a counselor to help me through the process. But the dark times helped me spiritually. I did shadow work and journaling. I started listening to my dreams and spirit guides that led me to fully embrace interconnectedness. I read all types of spiritual books, which further opened my heart and mind. I believe I was meant to be alone for part of my journey so I could see and understand spirit. Maybe being in a comfortable space wouldn't have pushed me to that realization. I also had to forgive myself for the mistakes I've made along my journey. If we can forgive ourselves, it makes it easier to forgive others.

I embrace Ho'oponopono, and use the technique anytime I make judgement. At first, I was amazed at how much I judged it was a real eye opener. The more I practiced, the less I judged, and the more it reinforced my belief in interconnectedness. I even have the saying printed on my phone case to remind me every day. Every time I make judgement, I say to myself, I'm sorry, please forgive me, thank you, I love you.

REMOVING BLOCKAGES

*N*egative thoughts were treated by Cherokee healers with the same medicines as wounds, headaches, or physical illness. It was believed that unchecked negative thoughts can permeate the being and manifest themselves in negative action
— Wilma Mankiller

How do you know you have blockages? When you keep re-living, on-going negative themes, when you get angry with certain circumstances, or continue with the same drama, you have blockages. What is your life reflecting? Do the same issues keep occurring? If they do, that is a blockage. Our life mirrors our personal beliefs and reflections, even if these beliefs are wrong. Some examples of being blocked are when you say no one likes me, I'm not good enough, I can't do it, it's not worth trying, I'm not smart enough, I'm not worthy, etc... You might feel resentment, self-sabotage, overreact, have depression, stress or fatigue. It weighs you down, impacts your mood, and you feel tired. You might feel tension or tightness in your body. You see these blockages all around you to validate your beliefs. Maybe your blockage is that you keep picking the same unhealthy friend or partner? Think about what negative programs keep coming back into your life.

Are your behaviors and identities holding you back? Do they no longer work for you? Were you ever told you were not enough or not lovable, and now live according to those expectations? Perhaps your family labeled you as being a perfectionist, klutz, lazy, or something else. Do not live your life according to a negative label. Don't hold on to old labels from others. Most self-limiting beliefs start from a young age and we reinforced them throughout our lifetime. It's time to re-evaluate in order to live your true path.

Some of us have experienced and still carry around pain from childhood. Our inner child may still be hurting. Your inner child is part of your subconscious mind that experienced and still remembers your childhood moments and emotions, both good and bad. If you experienced hurt in childhood, it is understandable that you lacked self-care skills at that time. How could you have taken care of him/her when you were just a child yourself? Now, you are strong enough to nurture your inner child. That is the beauty of getting older. We've learned how to take care of our mind, body, and spirit. Please don't underestimate yourself. You can start at this moment. Tell your inner child you are sorry for the hurt endured, and now you are here to protect him/her. Have a conversation and heal that part of yourself. Hug yourself daily and practice positive and loving self-talk. Reach out to a professional if necessary. You are worth it. Abandon anger and blame and simply love yourself. Stop trying to please the people in your life to gain self-approval. It's time to put your emotional attention and energy towards healing. Move forward and have the life you want instead of worrying about the past. The past is gone. Put the ghosts to bed.

We continue to live our lives according to the teachings and programming we received. We unconsciously follow those habits without being aware of any better alternatives. And we wonder why we are unhappy. We have no clue we live that way. For example, some people are still workaholics despite financial comfort. When you ask them why, they don't know. Someone instilled the habit in them as a child. Their parents' hard work to make ends meet still influences their belief, even though they have enough. Others have learned the drama lesson, making minor problems or emotions even bigger. Maybe you are playing the role of supermom or dad or perhaps the silent martyr role? We learn particular roles and don't even question why we are continuing to play that part. We mindlessly repeat the same routine, rarely questioning its effectiveness for ourselves or our loved ones. This is hard to overcome because we follow societal norms, and we get reinforcement or attention from others. It's important to re-evaluate your life to see if you have evolved past your old outdated labels. Ask yourself if the life you are leading right now is making you happy. If not, maybe it's time to re-evaluate.

Now that you understand about blockages and emotional wounds, how do you remove them? The following are three simple steps to help you on your Red Road journey. Despite their simplicity, implementing these teachings will require time and patience. There are many more techniques and resources available if you need further help.

The first big step is to recognize repeating negative scenarios that pop up in your life and realize they are indeed blockages. Think about your life and ask yourself what unpleasant themes and situations keep repeating themselves? According to the teachings of Bashar, you always move towards what you believe is beneficial and away from what you believe is painful. If you find yourself choosing the thing you know is more painful, it's an unconscious false belief, reinforced over time. He claims it is the sole reason for your unhappy choices.20

The second step after you recognize the blockage is to take time for self reflection. Assess where the blockage originated. Perhaps journalling or writing down past blockages will help you go deeper. Use the analogy of plant life. The healthiest plants have a good root system. Go deep and know what is hurting your roots in order to bloom. It's not to say you point and blame, you just become aware of what has been holding you back.

The third essential step is to eliminate the false narrative and claim ownership of your new belief. Your awareness allows you to evolve past your previous limited beliefs. It's not enough to recognize blockages and know where they originated. You must shift your beliefs and align with what works for you. Replace old beliefs and behaviors that no longer work for you with love, forgiveness, compassion, and strength. Be the change you want to see! Be the vibration you want to attract! Your journey can be powerful if you align with who you really are!

These three steps are a good start to help you become the person you were meant to be. There are many more techniques available, including holistic ones. Opening your heart chakra is a holistic teaching that can help you embrace compassion. When the heart chakra is unbalanced, you might experience feelings of isolation and the emotional pain of feeling unworthy. Simple exercises, like working with your breath, can balance your energy. Engaging in activities that expand your heart such as yoga, meditation, volunteering, walking in nature, or anything joyful or creative are great heart expanding exercises. Additionally, you can google chakra tests to assess the opening or closing of each chakra. The exercise might lead you to other spiritual teachings.

We want to reinforce the importance of compassion in removing blockages. When we have compassion for ourself and others, it allows us to understand our surrounding sacredness, knowing that we are all interconnected. Wouldn't it be great if we could all heal each other and our blockages by having our hearts filled with compassion and love? It would be so freeing.

You are ridding yourself of your blockages. Put your flaws and imperfections away in a drawer of your bureau. Why are you so quick to point them out? Embrace your strengths and remind yourself every day of them. Write them down, keep them close, and read them every day. You are enough; you are kind; you are special; you are made with purpose. Do you remember the scene in the movie "The Help" where the nanny kept repeating to the neglected girl, "You is smart, you is kind, you is important". Look in the mirror and repeat that. Studies have shown that positive affirmations can have a profound impact on our DNA. Research conducted by Bruce Lipton, a renowned cell biologist, proved just that. He stated that speaking positive affirmations for just

21 days can rewrite our DNA and change our gene expression. We're encouraging you to do the same. Write down positive affirmations and say them out loud every day in the mirror for 21 days. After the 21 days, you can keep the affirmations at your bedside to remind yourself of who you are meant to be.

Learn when critical individuals cross your path, they come to remind you of forgotten lessons on your spiritual journey. View it as a teaching, not a threat. Being non-judgmental is difficult. When you see yourself being critical, just catch yourself and change your perspective. Know that they have blockages too. Avoid making quick judgments about others. For example, a heavily tattooed person with piercings everywhere can bring automatic fear. Look how fast our heart can close. We look at the homeless and look away, cringe, or ignore them. No matter who you encounter, try to treat them with love and respect. We should treat everyone this way. When you enter a room without seeing ugliness, but with love in your heart, healing occurs. Healing is possible through the power of love. Great teachers have said this repeatedly.

Criticism runs rampant in our society. Why are we critical of ourselves and others? What about those critical individuals that keep showing up in our life? When people are negative, angry, critical, making poor choices, their hearts are hurting. Knowing this helps us to be more compassionate because we are walking the Red Road journey together. When people judge, they don't do it with their heart. When we remember this, we become less judgmental. We all come from unique life experiences and different perceptions.

Wouldn't it be amazing if all teachings came from the heart? We wouldn't have any blockages to remove if this were the case. But blockages can come from anywhere and everywhere. Our job is to chip away, making room for love and compassion while releasing anger and resentment. Ram Dass, a well-known author and spiritual teacher, talks about anger in his book, *Polishing the Mirror*. He says when he starts to get angry, he sees his predicament and how he is either getting caught up in expectations and/or righteousness. This teaching came from Maharaj-ji, who told him to polish the mirror free of anger to see God.21 This is a hard lesson, but observe your anger and ask yourself—is this because I have expectations or feeling righteous? Being a humble servant of God was the intended meaning of righteousness, instead of feeling superior to others. Somehow, we've turned away from the true meaning.

Some religious organizations that focus on division, ego, power, money, righteousness in order to control, demean and hurt others, have skewed from original teachings. Many are turning away from this focus. I believe people know their truth and understand that compassion, love, and gratitude are the essence of spiritual life. When we live in this way, we reach out beyond our suffering, our family and friends' suffering, and we touch on universal compassion, which is the highest form of compassion. We understand we are trying to live the best way we know how. It is this understanding that makes the world a better place.

The purpose of religion is to facilitate love and compassion, patience, tolerance, humility, and forgiveness. - Dalai Lama

Discover inner ways to share teachings and better yourself daily. Recall the Japanese saying masakatsu agatsu—victory or true victory over self. Create harmony by seeking inner awareness. When you bring those teachings to yourself, you will become self-disciplined every day, bringing victory to yourself and then to others. All things change when we do. Working on increasing our compassion will allow us to progress to higher levels.

Grandfather says: When you feel powerless, that's because you stopped listening to your own heart, that's where power comes from. — Gianni Crow

In summary, recognizing and removing your blockages help make room for more light and love in your heart. If your inner child is hurting, know you are strong enough to take care of him/her. Remove blockages by chiseling away, recognize anger and judgment as obstacles. Let go of past mistakes, labels, and hurts, and you can start to heal. Heal your heart, have compassion for yourself and others. Most importantly, write down how special you are and remind yourself daily! When you see negative, repeated patterns in your life, know it is a blockage. You don't have to align with that anymore. Don't get angry with it...it's there to teach you and help you grow, so please listen. Don't make any negative belief your own. Would Creator talk to you and have you believing that? Live your life with passion, creativity, joy, and love. Surround yourself with people who support you. Find your sacred space and know you are worthy. No matter what, people love you and you deserve respect and love.

Larry's Aha Moment

There was a time in my younger years that I felt I had to stick up for the underdogs. Although I thought I was protecting them, I was aggressive in my manner. It was a blockage because in my youth, I wanted someone to stick up for me. However, I realized it was the wrong tactic to take. Over the years, I learned to let go, forgive myself and others, and be the peaceful warrior by just walking away. I studied my native ways and other teachings that led me to be closer to Creator. Now my heart leads instead of the blockage in my head. Some people consider me a Wisdom Keeper, and I try my best to help people walk on the Good Red Road.

Pam's Aha Moment

In a previous chapter, I wrote about my estrangement from my parents. I worked extremely hard to release the blockage, even going to counseling and becoming a counselor to help me understand family issues. But even then, blockages can still raise its ugly head from time to time. My mom re-entered my life when I was 60. I was excited to finally experience love, thinking all that crap was behind me. I tried hard to prove myself, but our relationship and communication were still unhealthy. I realized after having surgery and cancer, I was physically and emotionally tired. I spent a month recuperating, reflecting, and isolating. I had the false belief that if I was good enough, I'd finally get the love that I yearned for. But I had a revelation. My aha moment finally happened! Even though I worked hard at chipping away at my blockage, it was here again to remind me I was good enough! There are no mistakes. Did I learn my lesson? Yes, and it didn't take long for my hurt to go away as I released my expectations. Reflecting on my life, I recognized the love of others and the good I've accomplished. It was my false belief, and it was my issue that resurfaced. Love exists between my mom and me, yet I've come to understand the need for self-love and letting go of expectations for anyone or anything in my life. That continues to be a humbling experience.

Don't forget to love yourself with all your heart. Remember that things resurface to remind you of your worth. Focus on what's working and those who love you. You are so loved.

EVEN MONKEYS FALL OUT OF TREES

If I had my life to live over again, I'd dare to make more mistakes next time.

— Nadine Star

Misfortunes do not flourish particularly in our path. They grow everywhere.

— Black Elk, Oglala Sioux (1863-1950)

This book contains many lessons. Trying to implement some of these teachings might make you feel overwhelmed. Know that you will make mistakes...we all do. Life is a journey, not a contest. Our job is to evolve and grow. There is not one person alive that's not made mistakes. People strive to be perfect, but perfection holds you back and is a barrier to your growth because it's an illusion. It doesn't exist.

There is a Japanese proverb, "Even monkeys fall out of trees," which means everyone makes mistakes. We strive to be an expert or a master, but it is just a matter of time before we fall to the bottom of the tree, scratching our head. Those are just the facts, little monkeys. We strive to present an impeccable image of ourselves. We want to share our accomplishments and good fortune with our loved ones, friends, coworkers, neighbors, and so forth. Who wants to share suffering? Who wants to share failures? When we scroll our friends' social network pages, do they show suffering? Does it show failures and disappointments? It usually depicts happy people and places having a fabulous time. Does that mean flaws don't exist in your friends, mentors, teachers, or neighbors? No, we all have failures and sufferings, but we hide them like dirty little secrets. We suffer alone. But separation and aloneness is a teaching that can help us awaken and transcend to a better understanding of who we really are. Our mistakes can be our greatest teachers.

The moment you know how your suffering came to be, you are already on the path of release from it. — Buddha

Thich Nhat Hanh emphasizes we must embrace suffering as a necessary part of our journey, urging us not to succumb to fear or flee from it. His belief is that if you allow fear to consume you, the path to peace and joy will remain out of reach. The Dali Lama states, "Suffering originates from various causes and conditions, but the root cause of our pain and suffering lies in our own ignorant and undisciplined state of mind. The happiness we seek can be attained only through the purification of our minds."22

Mistakes happen in our lives, but we need to take ownership of our mistakes. Reflect on your life and suffering. Are your negative beliefs, thoughts, and actions to blame for falling out of the tree? Is there something in your life right now that is a causing you a problem? If yes, your false belief may be the cause. Your life experiences are caused by your present beliefs. If you keep repeating the same mistakes and drama, change your thinking. How is your outlook? Do you look at the glass half-empty or half-full? Do you listen to the voices of others, or do you listen to your inner voice? How do you live your life? Do you let the energy of others dominate how you feel? Do you easily give up? Many inventors and business owners had many failures before success. For example, despite his brilliance, Thomas Edison's viable inventions only came after many trials and errors. A smart aleck reporter asked Edison about his many battery failures. Do you know his response? He said, "What are you talking about? Today, I am familiar with various methods of how not to manufacturing batteries"; he then asked the reporter, "What do you know? The question did not phase him. Did you know that Oprah Winfrey was once fired from her job as a news anchor? Look where she is now! Many successful leaders, inventors, and business owners have reinvented themselves and their products countless times. To assume their journey was effortless would be misleading. Ask any achiever and discover their shared trait—they didn't give up.

Realize that it is your decision how to handle your mishaps. The ball is in your court. Will you choose to learn from it or be upset? Don't misunderstand, it's normal to be upset. But do you become depressed, insecure, or give up? Now that's a problem. Don't keep being the victim. All life situations are here to help us evolve and to teach us spiritual lessons. Your repeated self-talk shapes your perception of yourself. If you keep saying I'm no good, I'm a failure, then you will believe it and live down to your expectation. Think back on your last mistake. What did you tell yourself? How can you change that thinking into something positive? A good exercise is what would you tell your child or a good friend if they failed? Treat yourself the same!

Reflect on your talents and joyful activities. Are you perfect at all of them? Do you need to be? Someone will always be better or worse. Are you familiar with the expression about the grass being greener on the other side of the fence? We jump the fence, but then we find out it's not greener. We're all in the same boat trying to do our best, but at times, our egos get in the way. That little voice inside our head that tells us we're failures if something doesn't work out. Embrace your resilience and let mistakes fuel your growth. You will reach higher levels of yourself when you try to do your best according to your abilities. When we are green, we grow; and when we are ripe, we rot. There may be times when we compete with ourselves and others to be perfect, and other times we don't even try because of low self-esteem, so we give up. Emotionally balanced individuals do not expect perfection because they understand it is impossible. Our point is to find your passion, do your best, and don't give up. Please do this exercise: Take a sheet of paper and write down all your accomplishments. Hang it on your mirror or keep it with you to remind you of all the wonderful things you have done and will continue to do! Mistakes are inevitable. We all make them and will continue to make them, but don't let that stop you!

Another obstacle that may hold you back is all or nothing thinking. For example, it's common to hear that either you're dieting or you fell off the wagon. As soon as you have that one extra cookie, you are off the diet, and you think you failed. You say to yourself, why not just eat whatever I want? I'm a failure. This thinking leaves no room for mistakes. Why not admit the error? I ate 20 cookies today and tomorrow is another day. Period. Don't sabotage yourself. It's easy to throw your hands up and give up. Thinking black or white is polarizing, and it doesn't allow us to see the middle ground. Life is about learning to navigate in the gray areas and putting your perspective in check. Nothing is all bad or all good.

For example, take a wedding. The bride's mother and the groom's mother both attended the wedding. Let's call one "Lucy" and the other "Ethel." Lucy thought it was an amazing wedding. Beautiful flowers, shining sun, and joyful dancing. Everyone had a great time. Nice wedding, right? Not so fast. Ethel said it was a terrible wedding. The food service was slow, Uncle George got into it with one guest, and to top it all off, the piano player was late. Now it was the same wedding, right? So which perspective is right? Both have chosen different perspectives - one positive, the other negative. How do you see your life? Do you always complain about your life despite its abundant blessings? Are you in the tree complaining about the other monkeys, their bananas, and how dirty the tree is and how bad the other monkeys smell? It's time to own your thoughts and life. Show yourself some kindness and avoid fixating on your gloomy thoughts. Just start looking at the positives. It will be difficult at first because you are in the habit of looking at the negatives, but we promise you...you will look at life differently if you change your perspective.

There are people that will criticize your mistakes but rarely acknowledge your accomplishments. So what? You don't have to take responsibility for other people's perceptions. People criticize for different reasons, but remember that they are imperfect as well. Remember the old saying, people in glass houses shouldn't throw stones. You don't have to join them in pointing out mistakes. Opt to empower others by highlighting their successes. When you look at your brother and sister, know they are not perfect—so be gentle, kind and encouraging. Even if you fall, remember the trees you've swung from and those surrounding you. It applies to everything in life. You can accomplish anything if you set your mind to it! We've talked about the Japanese term masakatsu agatsu, which means "true victory over self." We will all have moments where we fall out of the tree, and it is going to happen, but the true victory over self is when you make a mistake and you fall off the wagon, diet, or discipline, you bring it back into your practice.

Another important issue to address is mind reading. Know that you can't read people's minds, but we do that very thing! Much suffering and disagreements arise when people invent stories based on what they think another person is thinking. In our minds, we ruminate and concoct imaginary tales that bear no resemblance to what really happened. It causes so much drama and needless suffering. We must refrain from making up stories in our heads. Stop recycling and reprocessing every comment people make. When we do, we make a mountain out of a molehill, and blow things out of proportion. Maybe someone had a bad day or said something thoughtless, but it's rarely about you. Let it go and live your own story. Don't jump in where people are at. Use the analogy of stay in your own lane. If they have issues, that is their issues. Let it go. Their stories may evoke sadness, but yours can be different. You are not obligated to carry the weight of others on your shoulders. Their life lessons are not your life lesson. Let people play in their sandbox and don't join them. If they want to act childish, live in drama, or say immature things, that is their choice. Don't take it personal. You can choose how you react to things; that is your choice.

What about if someone is verbally attacking you? For example, what if someone cusses at you? A cuss word is just a word until you give it power. Are you that cuss word? Are you actually the person they are trying to make you out to be? This is not about you; it is where they are at. Is that person worth you getting upset, or worse, reacting? Do you want to act like them? If they're a good friend, address the upset tomorrow. Get your thoughts together, and then, if what you say is honest, kind, and true, communicate how you feel. Otherwise, just try to be the observer. A good exercise is to see the situation like you are watching a movie on TV. Being unattached about what is happening helps you to be non-reactive.

To summarize, we all fall out of trees. We all make mistakes, but one of our greatest lesson is to evolve, learn, and heal. The mistakes we make give us valuable lessons on courageousness and inner strength. Our journey should focus on kindness and patience with ourselves and others. So stand up, dust yourself off, and return to the tree.

Larry's Aha Moment

One thing that tweaked me was tailgaters. In the past, I used to get frustrated and slam on my breaks. I came to realize that I didn't want to be in that place anymore, so I tell myself that it is where I used to be, and now I choose not to react. Today, if someone is tailgating, I just turn my mirror. We want to react to situations. How do you know if you are reacting? If your breath and pulse are elevated, that is a good indicator that you are reacting. Wait until you calm down before you react. We are a reactive society. There are some people who are going to want you to react. They do things to get a reaction out of you, so don't let that happen. Don't give away your power.

What helps me not to react is my ceremonies. I face the east every morning to receive the blessings of the holy people as the sun rises. At a young age, we were taught that when the sun rises early in the morning, the holy people come out to give us their blessings. And that is when I talk to my spirit people to help guide me not to make all these mistakes. I give an offering of tobacco to all the sacred directions so that I can get reassurance from the people in the four sacred directions to help me in these endeavors. I have personal conversations with Creator every day, and he responds back to the whispers of the wind and he gives me a response on how to do these things and how much more I need to suffer to learn.

There are months and months when I don't make mistakes, and I feel, Oh my God, I'm living a great life, and then all of a sudden I get a reality check and mess up. I look at the mistake as what is the lesson in my own boo-hoos and why-me syndrome. I try to correct it and be better than yesterday.

Pam's Aha Moment

I've been there many times. Getting up is difficult after falling from the tallest tree. Sometimes I feel low and wish for a magic pill or an instant cure. What works for me when I'm down on myself is praying to my loved ones who have died and ask them to hold and comfort me. I know they are there for us if we ask. When I go to bed, I bring my guided meditation that brings forth healing. It's not magical, but little by little, I start feeling better, and I begin to unfold into the person I am meant to be.

This book is a good example of moving forward despite obstacles. I submitted this book to dozens of publishers and some replied with positive feedback but did not accept it for publication. Other publishers didn't take the time to respond. Yes, it was a disappointment, and it would have been so rewarding if they realized the book's worth. However, I reminded myself that I'm not a professional writer, nor do I want to be a perfectionist and take years to write a book. One year was enough for me. So, we decided to publish it ourselves.

Sometimes we take four steps forward and then two steps back. Why beat ourselves up for setbacks when we're actually moving forward? I was counseling a young man and in one of our sessions, he told me he felt so bad because he yelled at a person in front of his son. He was working on his anger issues and felt this was a setback. I asked him what he would have done last year if the same situation occurred. He said he would have punched the guy out. We both smiled because he realized he came a long way. Only dead people don't make mistakes. Treat yourself how you would treat a child. Wouldn't you be patient, kind, loving, reassuring, and forgiving? What makes you any different from that small child you want to nurture? Please forgive and be patient with yourself.

Larry and Pam

We've both fallen out of millions of trees. We could build a forest with the trees we've fallen out of. Love is our guiding principle and we aim to live in alignment with it, but we falter. The bottom line is that mistakes are going to be made. But always keep in the forefront of your mind that today is a new day. You can go to bed that night and wake up on a new day. You can be whoever you want to be today. Yesterday was gone. If you want, you can change your image or implement a new you. If you want to start by being compassionate and you weren't compassionate yesterday, then let that go and start all over again today.

One of the greatest teachings of the Dalai Lama is that you can become your own master. There is no teacher greater than yourself. While you can read this book and search for mentors, remember to listen to your heart. You know what to do. Go within—listen to your authentic voice, that is where your answers lie.

MANIFESTING

C reation said, "I want to hide something from the humans until they are ready for it. It is the realization that they create their own reality."

The eagle said, "Give it to me. I will take it to the moon."

The Creator said, "No. One day they will go there and find it."

The salmon said, "I will bury it on the bottom of the ocean."

The Creator said, "No. They will go there, too."

The buffalo said, "I will bury it on the Great Plains."

The Creator said, "They will cut into the skin of the earth and find it even there.:

Grandmother who lives in the breast of Mother Earth, and who has no physical eyes but sees with spiritual eyes, said, "Put it inside of them."

And the Creator said, "It is done."

— Creation story from the Hopi Nation, Arizona

We have explored various spiritual teachings to support us on our Red Road journey. Think of these teachings as necessary tools to aid in manifestation — the process of transforming ideas into reality. We all deserve to live our best life possible and manifesting our dreams does just that. Are you prepared to progress to the next level?

We hope you are clearing out unnecessary baggage and outdated beliefs that hold you back from living an authentic life. All things are possible when you make room to receive it. Creator intended for you to align with your soul's purpose and live your life in a joyful, creative, and passionate way. Understand that you've been manifesting all along by living and creating your own reality thus far in your life. You only need to refine and tweak how and what you are manifesting.

We will discuss 3 teachings necessary to help you navigate towards reaching your goals. There are many more techniques out there, but this is a good start. Mindfulness is the first teaching. By quieting your thoughts and aligning them in a positive, grateful, and loving manner, you can listen to the voices all around and within you. Teachers, in various forms, are waiting to help. They are always with you if you take time to listen. Mindfulness sounds simple, but it is difficult to master. Like anything else, it takes practice. If your brain is thinking about the future and/or past, you can not be in the present moment. If it's filled with all sorts of junk, there is no clarity or focus. All possibilities exist only in the present moment, therefore mindfulness can help you choose which possibility you want and act accordingly. Do you put gratitude into your morning routine or do you grab your cell phone, scroll Facebook and all your apps to feel connected? That is not mindfulness. You can say you want to be healthy, happy, free, and bring forth spiritual medicines, but you are programming the opposite. You need to be mindful of the difference.

Mindfulness is not meditating for hours a day. It can be simple activities such as crocheting, gardening, yoga, a walk in the woods, or even breathing techniques. You can also practice gratitude prayers and ceremonies to help clear and calm your mind. There are many mindful activities that you can explore. One great exercise is writing down mantras and spend a few minutes each day reciting them. A mantra is a word, or a series of words chanted aloud or silently. Some believe mantras are the first type of meditation that was developed. The goal with practicing mindfulness techniques is to help you connect with Creator and the Universal wisdom that guides you on your journey. When you stay present and attuned to your intuition, it makes you more receptive to synchronicities. Experiencing these synchronicities helps recognize that you're on the right path. Practicing mindful awareness and visualizing what you want also strengthens the vibrational alignment to your desired outcomes. Being mindful helps you release the old self that wasn't focused on your desired outcome. Your new self knows what it wants and will act on it. Are you seeing how the previous chapters are so important and why we left manifesting to last? You needed to gather your spiritual medicines first.

The second step to help you manifest is learning to prime your brain with new and clear intentions. So first mindfulness, then intention. Intention is the driving force behind the manifestation process and helps keep you in the right emotional state. Intent is determination, knowing what you want, and it needs to be clear. If your intent is unclear, it leads to vagueness. How can you create something that you can't define? Write down your intention and be specific and detailed. Intention gains its true power through the focus of your attention. For example, simply stating a desire to be happy lacks clarity. You must clearly define what your happiness looks like. According to Michael Losier's, *The Law of Attraction*, you attract into your life whatever you focus your attention and energy on, whether positive or negative. Know what you want and don't focus on what you don't want. Words have powerful vibration, so be precise and follow up with action.23

However, all your good intentions are just that — intentions. You need to solidify your intentions with thoughts, feelings, beliefs, and action. That makes them materialize. Believing you can do it is important, but belief alone is null and void if you don't have action. You can't just say, for example, "If the universe meant for me to have a man, I would have one". Girl, go out and be proactive by joining a group, attend a function, online dating, and keep your heart open. People think they make a wish and someone knocks on their door. What kind of person are you seeking? Be specific. Can you imagine that person with you? What would your life look and feel like? Feeling, imagining and asking for things you want is a great start, but you also have to act on it. If you feel unworthy of a good partner, remove that blockage within you. You might say you want a kind person, but date the bad guy or gal. Why is that? It's a blockage. Hopefully, you are aware of your blockages that have been holding you back. If you've met 50 Mr. or Ms. Wrongs, maybe you need to reassess? Be honest with yourself and look at your past patterns. There is always a lesson to learn in every encounter.

We previously discussed that we are co-creators vs passive observers. We can be action oriented just by understanding that fact. We are creating just by being alive and the universe responds to our belief. When we observe anything, we are making changes based on our observation. How powerful is that! Dr. Joe Dispenza, a renowned neuroscientist and author, emphasizes the power of our mind to shape reality by influencing the quantum field. Quantum experiments show that the focus of our attention can change reality itself and suggest that we live in an interactive universe. In addition, making choices in line with our future shapes our brain to be the person we aspire to become. Our universe actually changes and responds to us and our body chemistry changes too! He compares this phenomenon to computer programming. We recommend watching the video *Reprogram Your Brain in 7 days with Dr Joe Dispenza.24* or buy one of his many books. We are confident it will bring positive change to your life.

The third step is to be the vibration of what you want to attract to you. Practice mindfulness, set your intentions and now be the vibration of what you want to manifest. Everything is right there, ready to be chosen, but it won't manifest unless you align yourself to it. The universe does not give you what you want, it gives you WHO you are. So, work on being the partner you imagine yourself with, the employer, and/or friend. Be the person you want to be. Start breathing and living it, even if you're not already that person. Just by changing your thoughts and behaviors, you change your vibration. If you are stuck in negative drama or trying to force or predict an outcome, it stops positive results coming in. It's as if you are saying, no I don't want anything beneficial to come and I don't trust Creator or my synchronistic moments. I need to control every aspect of my being. When you have a negative or angry demeanor, that contributes to your vibration becoming smaller and your body tensing. How can you even see the possibilities? How can you be the possibilities? The quantum model of reality says when you are in the present moment with an open heart and no expectations, you broaden your vibrational field around you. Being heart centered opens you up to all the possibilities that exist, and then you can influence your reality. See how it all fits together? These teachings are all interconnected.

Think about how your body responds to your thoughts. When we have loving, grateful thoughts, we feel good and our body produces the feel-good chemicals of dopamine. Scientists have proven that our body produces chemicals and makes chemical changes depending on our thoughts. How exciting is that? When you are manifesting, you are changing everything about your chemical makeup. When you change your energy, you are changing your life. Bottom line is like attracts like. When you vibrate to something that is your same vibration, that is what you see and create. When you increase your vibration, you awaken to more opportunities and you tune in to what you want. Take a moment to think of people you know who manifest. They maintain unwavering focus and dedicate their mind, body, and soul to what they want, walking every step with purpose. They choose their own identity and embody it.

A good exercise to help increase your vibration is to practice being the observer. When you see something you don't like, don't get angry or judge it. Simply, don't choose it. When you like something, move towards it and take it into your form. Live, breathe and emote that which you want to vibrate towards. Don't put your attention on things you don't want! Let it go. Don't keep aligning with your problems. It keeps your vibration low, and you get stuck. Have you ever felt so overwhelmed by negativity that you feel stuck in mud, unable to move forward? You're unable to see the things that are right in front of you. Think about the people who always talk about things they hate — like politics, war, family drama, sickness, money problems, etc. They keep playing the same record over and over and it only draws more attention to it. It brings more of the same because you attract that vibration. How do you feel about these people? Do you feel like your vibration is increasing or decreasing? If you choose to only observe, experience, act, and behave with gratitude and abundance, that is what will come into your life. You are creating your experience because you are choosing what comes in and not reacting to what you don't want.

There is scientific evidence that suggests we are not only observers, but actual participators in the universe. The string theory proves communication goes beyond the realm of time and quantum entanglement states particles can be intimately linked, even if separated by billions of years. Gregg Braden, in his bestselling book, *The Spontaneous Healing of Belief: Shattering the Paradigm of False Limits*, talks of an experiment that demonstrates we are not merely observing, we are active contributors to everything that we see. In 1982, when the Lebanon and Israel conflict was taking place, researchers taught a group of people to feel peace in their bodies. Using the method of Transcendental Meditation, they taught the group to feel that peace was already present within them. They wanted them to feel peace, not just think or pray. They positioned the group in the geographical area of the conflict, and what they found was truly amazing — crime rates, emergency room visits and accidents all decreased in that region. This study showed that when a certain number of people achieved peace within themselves, it manifests in the geographical area! Next, the researchers identified the number of people required to share the experience of peace before it is mirrored in the world. The number is the square root of one percent of the population. So for a city of one million people, the number of people needed is about 100! In a world of 6 billion, it's just under 8,000 people needed to start feeling peace and begin the healing process.25 How powerful is that? We can literally change the world by feeling peace, by becoming the vibration of what we want to manifest.

Indigenous people understand the concept of feeling and being at peace without needing scientific evidence. The interconnectedness of all beings is a known part of their spirit. They know all things respond to spiritual vibrations and their ceremonies strengthened that belief. Everything has spirit, therefore it communicates. Participating with Creator and the universe through ceremonies, chanting, drumming, dancing, gratitude, etc...enhances alignment with spirit and it's a big part of who they are. It was and still is a shared and powerful experience.

In our society, we have a paradoxical paradigm. We have been raised to believe we are not powerful beings and have no effect on our world. With this belief comes apathy, believing we have no choice but to surrender to whatever circumstances we were dealt. We lose the understanding that Creator is part of us, just like Creator is part of the tree, the plant, the sky. Not believing that we are all interconnected, we become powerless. Slowly, the tides are turning with scientific studies, confirming that we do indeed have a shared field of energy with the universe. Fundamental shifts in beliefs are happening. Scientists are even identifying this field by names such as the quantum hologram, the mind of God, nature's mind, and the Divine Matrix.26

To summarize, how you think and feel creates your state of being. Practice mindfulness, set your intentions and be the vibration of what you want to manifest. Your past routines predict your future. Your subconscious memorizes sets of behaviors, attitudes, and perceptions. You are programmed because your routine is a habit. So it's important to change the operating system and act according to what you want to become. It's crucial to embody your desired vibration. Changing your habits and behaviors will be uncomfortable at first. People stay stuck because it takes work and focus. Be specific and commit, and keep remembering how powerful you are. Just knowing that you can influence and manipulate the outer world with your mind, what else are you capable of doing? Your mind's effect on matter creates boundless possibilities that shape your entire life. Now that's powerful!

Larry's Aha Moment

What I've thought about I became, and it started with my martial arts training. I struggled with dyslexia, so school was difficult for me. When martial arts entered my life, it disciplined me spiritually. It provided me with the foundation of mindfulness, intent and focus, which is important in manifestation.

I've also had great opportunities to learn from Wisdom Keepers. One in particular was Domingo (Ringo) Carrillo, who was an Elder in the State of Texas for the Lipan Apache Band. He knew the language, ceremonies, and had expert knowledge of Red Road teachings. I met him on one of the burial sites in Victoria where they unearthed 100 bodies of indigenous people, and he taught me and encouraged me to bring forth teachings.

There was no one in Corpus that stood up to the plate to do the teachings. I kept thinking, why don't we have the knowledge? Most of the Native Americans here were not raised on the reservation, so teachings were lost. I witnessed discrimination towards myself and my people and no one was bringing forth knowledge that all people so desperately need, and I said enough is enough. That's when we decided to do ceremonies in Corpus Christi, Texas that have not been done for 150 years.

I took up the cause because my heart was so aligned with the hurt of my people. I brought forth the teachings myself and more and more people kept asking for ceremonies and blessings. I had some people criticize, but I knew this was my heart and soul's purpose, so I ignored all the nay-sayers. I don't let anyone stand in my way. There were and are people that have negative feelings towards me and I just keep moving forward. I shut them down because my love for my people is so strong and this is about them, not me. This is how I manifested into a Wisdom Keeper.

Pam's Aha Moment

Working as a hospice nurse and counselor made me realize life is short. I heard so many times from my patients they were about to do this or that and then came the end of life. I took more chances in my life because of that lesson.

Before this book, not many people knew about my spiritual communication. How do you talk about a spirit guide called Clap Dance that delivers messages? I finally found the courage because I realize my soul's purpose is to share these encouraging messages.

I stay away from discussing scenarios that discriminate or divide people and I do not immerse myself in the news. Over time, I've learned that if I want my vibration high, I have to be part of the solution, not the problem. My life's purpose is now dedicated to inspire people to live in love and joy and to see the spirit in everything. My belief is that we are all interconnected, and everything else is an illusion. If you had one year to live, what would you aspire to do or become? Don't let fear, people, or insecurities stop your progress. Follow your passion. We all have insecurities, but visualize putting them in a draw and don't let it stop you from living. Think about what messages you would like to leave to your family, friends or community? This book is a manifestation of my and Larry's love and encouragement to leave behind for all of you reading. If these teachings help one person, it's all worth it!

CHANGING YOUR STORY

We want to leave you with the encouraging message that you can change your stories. You might be overjoyed with your current story, and we hope you have found this book uplifting to continue your journey with spirit. There might be moments when you're unhappy with your life circumstances. Perhaps you have felt, or will feel, isolated, alone, neglected, unappreciated, unconfident, or sad. We all have experienced undesirable life conditions where we find it difficult to move forward. We all need to take responsibility to change our story. Yes, life might have dealt you a bad hand, but blaming and complaining won't help. Our attitudes regarding life can either be a benefit or a detriment. We can stay stuck or fearful when we don't believe in ourselves or partner with Creator. It makes us sidestep off the Red Road. If this is where you are at this given moment, we hope that the spiritual teaching in this book will give you the strength to move forward. Remember, counselors and professionals are available to help you in any circumstance.

Let's use the analogy of your life to a book. Whatever situation you are experiencing now is just one chapter, out of many, in your book. There are many chapters before, many chapters after. If you could write your next chapter, knowing you have a choice to make life as you want, how would you write your next chapter? Please grab a pen and paper to answer the next four questions.

What direction do you want your life to take?

Which part of yourself do you wish to develop?

How can you change your behavior in order to accomplish what you want?

What steps can you take toward your life's path?

After reading this book, you might recognize that you may still be stuck in your story that you've carried over from childhood or other dramas and traumas in your life. Kudos for having the awareness to acknowledge that. It's the first step. You can't change your story without being introspective. We all forget and need reminding. This book provides tools to change your story if you choose. Your life will unfold to synchronistic events if you embrace and open your heart to the concepts in this book. Your energies can flow and you can step back on the Red Road with your spiritual medicines.

We're all brothers and sisters, each with a unique story. Wherever you are in your life, find your strength and partner with Creator. In this relationship, we acknowledge the power to improve daily. Remember, you are not alone. We are spirits having a human experience, and we are all interconnected. There is spirit in everything.

Walk in Creator's love and remember that every step you take is sacred. We love you.

Ishka,

Larry Running Turtle and Pamela Two Spirits

ABOUT THE AUTHORS

Larry Running Turtle Salazar is an American Indian of Tsalagi and Apache descent, and recognized as a Wisdom Keeper by his people. Larry's support of Native American issues includes documentaries, lectures, television appearances, radio host, and many other public arenas. Because of Larry's efforts, he has helped change laws in Texas pertaining to American Indian burial grounds. One of Larry's major quests is the pending construction of a monument on public lands of Corpus Christi to commemorate the location of the second largest Native American burial ground in the state of Texas. He is a member and advisor for South Texas Alliance of Indigenous People (STAIP).

Larry Running Turtle has performed countless ceremonies and continues to bring forth many lessons he has learned from life and from following the Good Red Road. Larry was trained in Japanese and Korean martial arts for over 48 years with 4 black belts from 4 different styles and also studied with Steven Seagal. This led him to a 10 year commitment to study and practice Buddhist teachings and eventually he met His Holiness The Dalai Lama and Thick Nhat Hanh. Larry is versed in the discipline of the Bushido, which embraces Eastern philosophy of peace, harmony, and respect for self and others. He believes in the correlation between Eastern, Native American, and other philosophies that embrace the respect of all life and existing in balance and harmony with Mother Earth. Larry is an Ambassador for the Goodwill Treaty for World Peace for the Indigenous Peoples's Grand Council of Peace. As is the obligation and commitment of a Wisdom Keeper to pass on his knowledge and wisdom, so Larry Running Turtle has dedicated his life to the inexhaustible teachings and guidance of all his apprentices and to all who choose to follow and practice the path of beauty, peace, and love.

Dr. Pamela Two Spirits Reader is a registered nurse with a master's degree in family sociology and a doctorate in transpersonal psychology. She has many years of nursing and counseling experience, mostly with hospice, working with patients and their families to help loved ones cross over. Pamela has explored many spiritual concepts, including studying meditation with Buddhist monks which led her to become a hypnotherapist and Reiki practitioner. During her lifetime, she has had many dreams with a Native American spirit guide named Clap Dance that has helped her to connect with the concept of interconnectedness. She has produced a hypnotherapy CD called "Loving Energy," based on a dream she experienced as a molecule in a drop of water with her spirit guide. The program helps people heal on a physical, emotional, and spiritual level and can be found on YouTube.

Pam and her husband, David, live in North East Florida. They own a house on the St Johns river where they spend their days fishing, boating, and gardening. Pam is happiest living a quiet life surrounded by trees, water, and nature. Fishing, boating, hiking, and photography are her passions.

Pam and her co-author Larry Running Turtle met over 20 years ago and realized their lessons and teachings were in the same voice, with one heart. They made their relationship official by having a sacred brother and sister ceremony. Larry presided over Pam and David's wedding, as well as her naming ceremony. Their belief is that we are all interconnected, and their hope is to give that message to all who will listen. They believe spirituality should not be illusive or difficult to obtain. Their mantra is that we don't need to look far and hard for spirituality because it exists within and around us. Their hope is that people will embrace the simple teachings of this book and to remember that we are all spirits having a human experience.

EPILOGUE

M odern Warriors and Bureaucratic Ways. As a Native American who grew up in the Native ways, I know the history of how our ways were taken away from us. They forcefully took away our natural ways, the quiet life, and all the purity of the earth at gunpoint. Colonizers stripped away our culture, families, and land, and forced us to become the people they wanted us to be instead of embracing our authentic selves, as Creator intended. They took away all these things from us, including our land and mineral rights, our freedom of speech and religion. On August 11, 1978, the Freedom and Religion Act became law and granted us the ability to worship as we were intended.

Bureaucratically, these things are still happening to us. Now the talking drums of our people today are the briefcases, cell phones, and computers in order for us to communicate with other nations and tribes around the world. These are our weapons now—the ones that they educated us on. Native Americans once had that silent world, the pure unadulterated waters. We walked our own sacred ground connected to its essence and beauty.

We once had all that in abundance, but they stripped it away. Now we watch the same people grow tired of their own world as they go into the forest and parts of the country where no one has stepped foot. They want to build their condos and homes and call it peaceful and beautiful, and that is fine, but they have no regard for Mother Earth or her children. Modern men build without realizing the surrounding sacredness. They take without replenishing.

The way we connect with people, the way they have educated us to do these things, is with technology. I am a spokesman, and everyone wants to know what is going on and how quickly we can respond to the burial ground that is being stripped away inch by inch in the name of development. The cell phones are now necessary because we must be warriors of the modern world, and we need to have our warriors ready to act accordingly as far as protesting is concerned to stop atrocities that are still taking place today. Before, it was shooting people and forcing them to move from their homeland. Even the bureaucracy of today is embedding our own people with mixed blood by saying I'm one-fourth this or three-fourth this, like comparing us to dogs or horses. We are not measured in cups, so this is a bureaucratic way of genocide. Sooner or later when we can't prove our quantum of blood, we won't exist in their eyes. Why is it we are the only race among humanity who needs to prove by our quantum of blood the way we live or choose to live?

These are the bureaucratic ways we have to stop. Now we use their technologies to contact media and the newspeople to remind them these things are still happening. We get to witness this as they slowly strip away our lands and our sacred sites that are taken over because they want our mineral rights and what is underneath our peoples' bones by oil, gas, water, or whatever is left beneath the earth. As if it is not good enough to take what is on top of the earth, they have to take what is underneath it as well. They reach deep in the core of Mother Earth and strip her away of her essence. So we now have the power to contact people within our people who know the mineral right laws, and we need these talking phones and quick lines to be able to stop and enforce these laws.

I understand the quiet and simple life and walking and living with nature. We were there once, and it is good to come back to our relatives in these ways. However, to remain vigilant, we become connected to the modern things that bind us to the world. It seems that as soon as we put them down and shut them off, another burial site was just violated or more mineral rights were pulled out of the Indian Reservations. The media and the government are always willing to communicate these things to you. How can we conduct ceremonies and meetings to get people to stop these things? The government does not stop just because you are asleep or stepped away, and they will not stop until they have everything they can possess. The worst thing they ever did to our people was not the killing or annihilating us, it was educating us because now we have their own weapons and we are now at their level of education, so we can put a stop to these things. We can talk about our spiritual teachings and connection to Creator, Mother Earth and her children is in this book. This is the world I live in now, and this is my way of going to battle and protecting my people. These are my connections to the sacred people. I get calls all over Turtle Island asking me for prayers and medicine, and I do the same thing and reach out to them because I can reach out to them because of technology. This is the advantage of technology. People and the sacred people call me a Wisdom Keeper, but I'm just a modest person trying to bring forth teachings that people have forgotten.

Larry Running Turtle Salazar

We will be known forever by the tracks we leave. — Dakota Proverb

How Christ Appeared to Our People

This is the story that my mom shared with me, (remember the Mexican/Catholic lens I mentioned earlier), and the Mormon's Bible confirmed part of the story—not that I am a Mormon. This is the way the story goes I hold true to my heart. Over two thousand years ago, when Christ was entombed after his crucifixion, the question was asked, "Where was he?" The answer was that he went to all nations all over the world, and he appeared to different people in different forms in different ways. When he appeared to our people on Turtle Island, he showed up in spirit wearing white regalia, which were made of an albino elk hide. The first thing he did when he appeared to our people was to hold up his left hand to show his stigmata wounds. When he spoke, he spoke in a language that we all understood. He stated he had been crucified, and that he was the son of the Holy Father.

Christ told our people that he left many teachings on the other side of the world, and that in the future people would be coming to the new world to bring forth all his teachings, and that was the reason they were going to come to Turtle Island. He asked us to look out for his children when they were sailing across the ocean. We would recognize that they were his children because they were going to come in wooden boats with the sign of the cross on their sails and around their necks as well. They were going to be carrying these enormous books with all the lessons and parables that he left behind in the old world that he wanted to be shared among our people in the new world. He asked us to welcome his children, embrace them, cherish them, nurture them, feed them, and then send them back on their way. Then he ascended back into heaven.

Sure enough ships started coming in just like Jesus described, and in fact they had crosses on their sails, and the old ones got together in counsel and said this is one prophecy that were given to us by the white God and how are we going to greet these people. One elder said, "Let's greet them like Christ greeted us with our left hand raised." Hollywood has depicted that as the sign of "How" as a greeting. But in fact, it was our interpretation of the sign of Christ and how he appeared to our people. The left hand, to our people, is the most sacred because it is closest to our heart.

However, we soon learned that something became very deceiving of these new people. They did have enormous books in their left hand, but in their right they had a musket gun with long swords. They also noticed they had these deep empty pockets ready to fill up with all the treasures, jewels, and gold they saw our people wearing. And they wanted more of these things, so they started slaughtering, killing, taking more than they needed, raping our land and our loved ones of their treasures. We were deceived, just like the white God was deceived. As more and more of these ships came in raping our land, we knew that in our hearts there were still a lot of good in a lot of these people, and most came for good and right intentions, but the others came in with an abundance of greed. So we started a war against these people, and as time went on, the warriors would come to the medicine man and holy man to ask for a blessing before war or before they hunted. The holy and medicine man would dip their hand in red paint and mark the warriors on their face or on their chest or their horses so the horses could take them and bring them back in a good way or for plenty of game for the people. They did this in remembrance of Christ.

But as time went on, the game was becoming less and less because the white people cut off our food sources by eliminating all our buffalo. They eliminated all our crops because they burned it all down. But we have never forgotten the teachings of the white God or the way he appeared to us. We hold that dear to our hearts and the sign of Christ by holding up our left hand.

THE ISHKA SACRED SITE

How We Got Our Start. It all began in 1994 when Larry Running Turtle Salazar was notified about the discovery of ancient bones found under Ennis Joslin Rd and Alameda Rd. He blessed the bones of the young girl and vowed that as long as he was on this earth, he would find a way to honor her and others found at the site 41NU2 (the location of the 2nd largest Native American burial site in Texas).

Larry set out to commemorate the burial site, bringing more awareness to the community about the site. This effort took many turns including renaming the street where the ancient bones were found to building a monument commemorating the site. Over the years there were various setbacks, but his determination never wavered and today the project has evolved into a more dynamic project that will not only honor the ancestors of the land, but will provide much more for the community.

The Full Story. The Ishka Sacred Site is supported by the South Texas Alliance of Indigenous People (STAIP) and is a 501(c)3. Please see ishkasacredsite.org[1]

STAIP's mission:

---

1. http://ishkasacredsite.org

Create a space to honor the rich Native American history, past and present in the Coastal Bend, connect to Spirit and nature, increase public awareness while also supporting and embracing Indigenous heritage through education.

Our vision
- Create a better space for future gatherings.
- Provide a space for the community to learn about and embrace their heritage
- Provide a place for Native Americans and all people to conduct their ceremonies, both locally and afar.
- Give Park users from all walks of life an opportunity to learn about the ancient history of the land
- Revitalize the local Lipan Apache language through graphics and an app

- Provide a burial vault to repatriate remains dug up from the surrounding area

The creation of STAIP's 501(c)3 status was spearheaded by Larry Running Turtle Salazar under the umbrella of the Center for Progressive Studies and Culture, a non-profit that supports small, local grass roots non-profits.

The Proposal. The vision for the Ishka Site is to create spaces on this natural setting in which to honor the First People of the Coastal Bend, increase public awareness of indigenous culture, offer unique experiences and recreational opportunities, and show the connection between Native American spirituality, well-being, and nature. It would be an inclusive space for all people to experience.

Site Location. The proposed Ishka site would be located in the south-eastern end of Hans and Pat Suter Wildlife Refuge where a Medicine Wheel is already in place and where there are plans to install a statue of a Native American. Besides the Medicine Wheel this area currently includes a small parking lot, a playground, open fields which have been used for dancing and teepees, and two access points to Oso Bay

Site Description for the Ishka Experience
- A Statue of a Native American Man
- A 20 ft Gathering Circle
- A 30 ft Gathering Circle
- 10 small Shade Structures
- 50 Laser-cut Corten Steel Informative Panels
- 40 Benches
- 10 to 20 indigenous Bronze animals
- Large Laser-cut Corten Steel Entrance Sign
- Additional Parking lot and Path Extension

A burial vault to repatriate disturbed remains from the archaeological site will also be placed at the site

The Statue. A physical symbol of Native American spiritual expression, the bronze Statue will represent a native man who might have lived by Oso Bay. His clothing would be a loincloth and his hair would be in braids. Larry Running Turtle Salazar tells us, "We get our blessings from the holy people right as the sun is rising. The statue will face East with the left hand raised to the rising sun while offering tobacco to the holy people. Slightly larger than life-size and resting on a low pedestal of rocks and plants, the statue would be approachable to touch. He represents thousands of years of different tribes who lived in the Coastal Bend. The Statue would be located in an Orientation Area just beyond the small parking lot.

The Panels. Approximately 50 Corten Steel laser-cut Panels will support the roofs and provide the walls for the Structures. The Panels will rust after installation as they become exposed to the environment. This will provide corrosion resistance lasting decades. The Panels will depict topics relating to nature, local indigenous history, and spirituality. Some of the text would have Apache translations. An App is being planned to enable the user to listen to spoken Apache while viewing selected Panels.

The Gathering Circles. The Gathering Circles provide spaces that encourage Ceremonies and Gatherings for all groups - large or small. They would be located across the field from the medicine wheel leaving room for dancing and teepees or other activities. They would also tempt visitors to linger and read the panels or sit on a bench to enjoy the shade and the space. The Gathering Circles have several Openings by which to enter the space. They each have an opening facing East, the traditional entrance in Apache and other Nation's cultures.

The Shade Structures. Each of the ten Shade Structures would include 3 panels and a bench. The roof rafters would arch upwards towards a partial oculus in the center. Three of the Shade Structures would be located in the Orientation Area around the statue (beyond the existing small parking lot) and provide maps and information. The other Shade Structures would be themed and set in appropriate spots throughout the area.

Benches Benches are part of the Structures and most would be set within the shade patterns. Made of recycled plastic, the benches would last for decades. Curved benches were selected to continue the curved lines in the structures.

Bronze Animals. The plan is for 10 to 20 bronze sculptures of indigenous animals to be scattered throughout the site. Child friendly and sized for sitting, they would be educational and a fun challenge for a child to find and identify them all. The panels in Shade Structures by the Playground would relate to the animals. Like the Bronze Sculpture, the bronze animals would not be waxed or patinated. They would naturally oxidize in the air to a harmless patina coating which protects the inner layers of the bronze. There is no need for yearly polishing.

The Entrance Sign. The large Entrance Sign would be similar to the Corten Steel laser-cut panels used throughout the site. It would be close to Ennis Joslin Road next to the driveway and would be in a setting of cactus or other native plants. Titan-cut, the manufacturer of the Panels, would provide lighting so the cut-out letters would be visible at night.

ishkasacredsite.org[2]

---

2.   http://ishkasacredsite.org

ENDNOTES

1. John Redtail Freesoul, *Breath of the Invisible* (A Quest book 1986), 9.
2. Alan Watts, *In My Own Way: An Autobiography* (California: New World Library, 1972). P. 4
3. Masaru Emoto, *The Hidden Messages in Water* (Hillsboro Oregon, Beyond Words, 2004).
4. Kevin J. Tokeschi, *Edgar Cayce on Vibrations: Spirit in Motion* (A.R.E. Press, 2007), 262-127 report.
5. Carl G. Jung (1960), *Synchronicity: An Acausal Connecting Principle*, (Princeton University Press, 2012) p. 44
6. Kevin J. Tokeschi, *Edgar Cayce on Vibrations: Spirit in Motion* (A.R.E. Press, 2007), 262-127.
7. John Poupart and John Red Horse, *To Build a Bridge: Working with American Indian Communities*, (American Indian Policy Center, 2000)
8. Anna Breytenbach, "Black Leopard and The Animal Communicator," YouTube Video, March 6, 2014, 0:12 - 8:32, https://www.youtube.com/watch?v==wL—zc1Klxk.
9. Thich Nhat Hanh, *The Heart of the Buddha's Teaching* (Berkeley, California Parallax Press, 1998), 137.
10. Ed McGaa Eagle Man, *Mother Earth Spirituality: Native American Paths to Healing Ourselves and Our World* (New York, Harper Collins,1990), 41.
11. Freesoul, *Breath of the Invisable*
12. Eckhart Tolle, *A New Earth: Awakening to Your Life's*

Purpose (New York, Penguin, 2005), 32.

13. Tolle, *A New Earth*
14. Hanh, *The Heart of the Buddha's teaching,* 10-11
15. Stephanie Dowrick, *Choosing Happiness: Life and Soul Essentials (New York, Penguin, 2005), 53.*
16. Hanh, *The Heart of the Buddha's Teaching,* 10–11.
17. Stephanie Dowrick, *Choosing Happiness*
18. Ulrich E. Dupree, *Ho 'oponopono: The Hawaiian forgiveness ritual as the key to your life's fulfillment* (Earthdancer, 2012)
19. Mother Teresa of Calcutta, *A Gift for God: Prayers and Meditations* (New York, Harper Collins, 1996).
20. Richard Gentle, *Seth, Abraham, Bashar!* (UK, Keekoo Publications, 2022) P
21. Ram Dass, *Polishing The Mirror: how to live from your spiritual heart (Boulder, CO. Sounds True, 2013) P.* 55
22. Hanh, *The Heart of the Buddha's Teaching*
23. *Law of attraction: The Science of Attracting More of What You Wand and Less of What You Don't (*Wellness Central, 2010)
24. Dr Joe Dispenza, "Reprogram Your Mind in 7 Days with Dr. Joe Dispenza," YouTube Video, November 13, 2023 0:02 - 1:32, https://www.youtube.ocm/watch?v=KvyyGsTPvvM.
25. Gregg Braden, *The Spontaneous Healing of Belief: Shattering the Paradigm of False Limits* (Carlsbad, CA: Hay House , 2008) p 48
26. Gregg Braden, *The Divine Matrix: Bridging Time, Space, Miracles, and Belief* (Carlsbad, CA: Hay House, 2007):p. 54

www.ingramcontent.com/pod-product-compliance
Lightning Source LLC
Chambersburg PA
CBHW060528150626
46553CB00024B/1686